O9-ABE-335

CULTURE SMART!
HUNGARY

Brian McLean

·K·U·P·E·R·A·R·D·

ISBN 978 1 85733 335 0
This book is also available as an e-book: eISBN 978 1 85733 599 6

British Library Cataloguing in Publication Data
A CIP catalogue entry for this book is available from the British Library

First published in Great Britain
by Kuperard, an imprint of Bravo Ltd
59 Hutton Grove, London N12 8DS
Tel: +44 (0) 20 8446 2440   Fax: +44 (0) 20 8446 2441
www.culturesmart.co.uk
Inquiries: sales@kuperard.co.uk

Distributed in the United States and Canada
by Random House Distribution Services
1745 Broadway, New York, NY 10019
Tel: +1 (212) 572-2844 Fax: +1 (212) 572-4961
Inquiries: csorders@randomhouse.com

Series Editor Geoffrey Chesler
Design Bobby Birchall

Printed in Malaysia

Cover image: Széchenyi thermal baths, Budapest.
Travel Ink/David Forman

Image on page 27 reproduced under Creative Commons Attribution-Share Alike 3.0 Unported license: © I, Guilherme Paula

About the Author

BRIAN McLEAN is a British translator and journalist. He spent periods in Japan and Austria before settling in Hungary in 1977. He is the author of *Escape Routes: Ten Excursions from Budapest*. He has translated about fifty, mainly scholarly, books, including Gabriella Balla's *Herend* (an illustrated history of the porcelain factory), *Political Economy of Socialism* by János Kornai, and *The Holy Crown of Hungary* by Endre Tóth and Károly Szelényi.

contents

contents

Map of Hungary

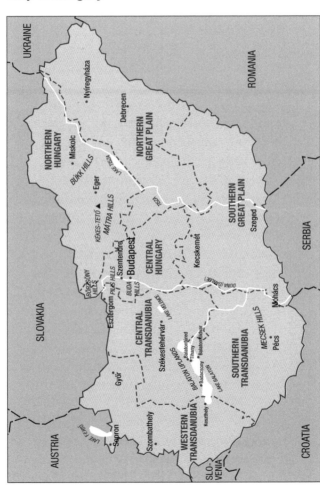

introduction

Hungary's reputation for hospitality dates back a thousand years. St. Stephen, the country's first king, wrote in the early eleventh century, "Visitors and newcomers bring such gain that they may worthily stand in sixth place in royal dignity." The Hungarian belief in the importance of learning from abroad has changed little, too, and this combination of good-natured openness and self-respect is a very attractive Hungarian trait.

This is worth emphasizing especially because of Hungary's recent history. From the end of the Second World War until 1990, Hungary was part of the Soviet bloc, that Eastern Europe of workers, tractors, factories, drab clothes, and dull streets. Today Hungarians feel part of Central Europe again, the Europe that once belonged to the Habsburg empire, full of Baroque churches, and sturdy nineteenth-century schools, town halls, barracks, and railway stations, such as you might find anywhere between Bosnia and the Czech Republic, Austria, and Romania.

In a religious and intellectual sense, Hungary lies north and west of the dividing line between Catholic/Protestant Europe and Eastern Orthodox Europe. Now there's another division running through Hungarian society. It's like the old divide in France between Catholic and anticlerical. The two strands were known here in the 1930s as *nép-nemzeti* and *urbánus*, which today translate into "conservative" and "liberal." Many are dismayed to see this division back, but it's best to be aware of it. Churchgoing, choosing a school, even going to a film or a play is a more political act than in English-speaking countries.

So what are modern Hungarians like? Paradoxical, you could say. They are talkative, but reticent; they are voluble, amusing, and full of an irony verging on cynicism. But beneath the self-denigration lies a strong confidence in their own culture, way of life, and achievements against all the historical odds. This faith in themselves is a private matter that they may not like to bother you with. They love to solve problems and overcome a crisis, but they may lose interest when everything's running smoothly. They are cheerful, but doleful. There's fatalism mixed into the optimism, and resentment found among the pride. There's no easy way to sum up the fascinating complexity of the Hungarian character. Knowledge, the key to understanding, is what *Culture Smart! Hungary* sets out to provide. Read on, and enjoy the journey!

Key Facts

Official Name	Republic of Hungary/ *Magyar Köztársaság* (since 1990)	Hungary joined the E.U. on May 1, 2004.
Capital City	Budapest. Pop. 1.7 million	Buda, Pest, and Óbuda merged in 1876.
Other Main Cities	Debrecen, Miskolc, Szeged, Pécs, Győr	
Area	35,919 sq. miles (93,030 sq. km)	
Climate	Temperate, with changeable weather. The climate gets drier and more extreme from W to E.	
Currency	Hungarian forint Paper: 200, 500, 1000, 5000, 10,000, 20,000. Coins: 100–1.	
Population	10,097,945 (est. 2005)	Density: 281 per sq. mile (109 per sq. kilometer)
Ethnic Makeup	Almost all see themselves as Hungarian, some also as Roma (Gypsy, 4–6%), German (2.1%), or Slovak (1%), etc.	Some 1.5 percent of population are foreign nationals.
Language	Hungarian (Magyar) is the official language and first language of 98.5%.	English and German are the main foreign languages taught in schools.
Religion	55% describe themselves as Roman Catholic, 15% Reformed Protestant, and 3% Evangelical (Lutheran). Almost all denominations receive state support.	

Government	Parliamentary democracy (since 1990) with single-chamber parliament. Half the legislature elected by constituencies and half by a list system. The head of state is the president. The head of government is the prime minister.	Local government, mayors, and European MPs elected by residents. The 7 E.U. regions cover 19 counties, Budapest, and 22 cities with county status.
Hungarians Abroad	Some 5 million Hungarians live abroad (3 million in neighboring countries, within pre-First World War "historical" Hungary).	Large Hungarian communities exist in the U.S.A., Germany, Canada, etc., but rapid assimilation makes them hard to quantify.
Media	3 TV and 3 radio state-controlled stations; 2 national commercial TV networks; 4 main national dailies, 1 free daily, 2 financial dailies, several tabloids and provincial dailies.	Budapest has 2 English weeklies and 1 German. The news agency MTI and others provide wire, Internet, and newsletter services in English. No local broadcast media in English at present.
Electricity	220 volts and 50 Hz with standard European plugs and sockets.	U.K. appliances need adapters, U.S./Canadian transformers too.
TV, Video, and DVD	PAL B system. Not compatible with U.S. videos, and only with Region 2 DVDs	
Internet Domain	.hu	
Telephone	Hungary's country code is 36.	To dial out, dial 00 for international, 06 for domestic trunk and mobile calls.

chapter one

LAND &
PEOPLE

"Hazám, hazám . . . "
"Homeland, my homeland, my all! My whole
life I owe to thee," sings the troubled medieval
patriot Bánk bán in the eponymous 1860 opera
by the Hungarian composer Ferenc Erkel. You
won't meet a Hungarian who disagrees. People
from larger countries may sometimes take theirs
for granted, but not people from smaller, more
vulnerable countries like Hungary. Patriotism
there runs as deep as deep can be.

GEOGRAPHICAL MATTERS
Hungary is a landlocked country in the center of
Europe. Budapest, the capital, lies about 890 miles
(1,425 km) from London, 980 miles (1,575 km)
from Moscow, 500 miles (800 km) from Rome,
and 655 miles (1,050 km) from Istanbul, as the
crow flies. Hungary's area of 35,919 square miles
(93,032 sq. km) makes it similar in size to
Portugal, or to the state of Indiana. It has an
irregular egg shape.

Hungary occupies the center of the large, relatively flat Carpathian Basin. It is surrounded by the Alps, the Carpathians, and the Dinaric Alps, but none of these ranges extend into Hungary, where the highest point—the peak of Kékes-tető, 60 miles (95 km) east of Budapest—is only 3,326 feet (1,014 m) above sea level. Going clockwise, the countries across Hungary's 1,377 miles (2,217 km) of frontier are Austria, Slovakia, Ukraine, Romania, Serbia, Croatia, and Slovenia.

The Danube, Europe's second-longest river after the Volga, arrives from Slovakia and follows the border east, before turning due south to bisect the country and enter Serbia. The part of Hungary to the west of it is called Transdanubia *(Dunántúl)*. To the east lie the Northern Uplands *(Északi hegység)* and the Great Plain *(Alföld)*.

Transdanubia has three major lakes, all shallow and fringed with reeds. The largest by far is Balaton (232 square miles or 600 sq. km). The second largest is Fertő (Neusiedlersee), which straddles the border with Austria. Between Balaton and Budapest lies Lake Velence.

The main ranges of hills in Hungary form an almost straight line from southwest to northeast, from the Balaton Uplands to Buda Hills and continuing on the opposite side of the Danube as the Northern Uplands. The western border with Austria runs through Alpine foothills.

The population of Hungary peaked at around 10.7 million in 1981 (similar to that of Ohio or Illinois), but since then it has fallen by an estimated 5.5 percent to around 10.1 million in 2005. The population density of 279 per square mile (108 per sq. km), is less than half that of Germany or the U.K., but over three times that of the U.S.A. Only Central Hungary (Budapest and Pest County) has a population density well above average, at 1,056 per square mile (408 per sq. km).

CLIMATE AND WEATHER

Hungary is said to have a temperate climate, but you could be fooled sometimes. The variability of the weather is explained by the position of the country, at the junction of the Maritime, Continental, and Mediterranean climatic zones. There seems to be a trend toward greater variation within the country, and from year to year, in both temperature and rainfall.

Hungary has a mean annual temperature of 50°F (just under 10°C), with strong variation from year to year. The mean temperature is hottest in July (68°F, 20°C) and coldest in January (35°F, 2°C), but these averages may include hot days at 90–100°F (33–38°C) and cold nights at -15–20°F (-26–29°C), respectively. Local mean annual temperatures in 2004 ranged between 42°F (5.4°C) on Kékes-tető and 53°F (11.7°C) in Szeged. The trend over the last thirty years has been slightly upward, in line with global warming.

Rainfall is variable too. The annual mean ranges from 28–32 inches (700–800 mm) in the west to 18–22 inches (470–550 mm) in the Great Plain. Yet 1999's nationwide mean of 31 inches (775 mm) was followed in 2000 by only 16 inches (400 mm). The pattern of rainfall is far from ideal. Much of it comes in summer thunder-storms, so it quickly runs off or evaporates. This leaves parts of the Great Plain arid, with some shifting sand dunes to the west of Kecskemét.

Snow does not usually fall before November or after April. A group of English people used to celebrate Guy Fawkes night (November 5) with fireworks in a Budakeszi garden, but they gave it up, as it usually coincided with the first bout of really cold weather. A continuous period of snow cover and daytime frost is likely in December, January, and/or February.

Many Hungarians suffer from headaches or other symptoms as warm or cold weather fronts pass over. Suggestion is a powerful force, and foreigners living in Hungary soon become sensitized in the same way.

The prevailing wind in Hungary is from the northwest. There are about 2,000 hours of sunshine a year.

Badacsony, overlooking Lake Balaton, is one of several obvious extinct volcanoes in Hungary, but there are no active ones today. No earthquake recorded in the territory of present-day Hungary has had a magnitude greater than 6 on the Richter scale. The last earthquake fatality was in 1956 at Dunaharaszti, south of Budapest, when a makeshift house collapsed.

A BRIEF HISTORY
Before the Hungarians
The first written references to the area known as Hungary today date from the fifth century BC. These, and archaeological evidence, suggest that Celtic tribes arrived about 400 BCE and controlled the area of modern Transdanubia—Hungary to the west of the Danube. Celtic culture in Hungary is thought to have been at its height toward the end of the third and into the second century BCE.

Rivalry with Illyrian, Dacian, and other tribes weakened the Celts. By about 12 BCE the Romans had established their rule over the area of

modern western Hungary,
which became part of the
Roman province of Pannonia.
There are some spectacular remains,
for example in Budapest (Aquincum)
and near Székesfehérvár (Gorsium).

In 361 CE the Romans, their empire
in decline, invited the troublesome,
warlike Huns to settle in Pannonia, but the rule of
their famous leader Attila was brief. There
followed successive conquests of the area over
more than five centuries, by Ostrogoths, Gepids,
Lombards, Avars, and Slavs, before the
Hungarians arrived.

The Magyars

With no written historical records for guidance, it
is hard to say exactly where the Magyars or
Hungarians came from. Linguistically, Hungarian
belongs to the Finno-Ugric group of languages
(see Chapter 9), the other surviving members of
which occur in Northern Scandinavia and in
pockets around the Baltic and across the territory
of present-day Russia.

The split between the Finnic and Ugric tribes is
usually dated to around 500 BCE, by which time
the latter were pursuing an agricultural as well as
a pastoral lifestyle, breeding horses and using
iron. Their cultures were strongly influenced

during the first millennium CE by tribes of Iranian origin and by neighboring Greek, Persian, and Armenian cultures.

By the fifth century AD, the Hungarians can be distinguished from other Ugric tribes and were in close contact with Bulgar Turks, on the steppes flanking the River Volga. An Arab source of the period remarks that the Hungarians "have tents and move to find fresh grass and lush vegetation." They were part of successive loose federations of tribes, notably the Khazars.

By the ninth century, the Hungarians were centered further west around the River Dnieper and taking part in the political struggles among the Slavs and the Eastern Franks for control of the middle Danube Basin. The Hungarians do not seem to have met any effective resistance when they invaded the Carpathian Basin at the end of the ninth century, united under Árpád, chief of the Magyar tribe. (Traditionally, seven tribes of warlike, pagan, seminomadic Magyars, headed by Árpád, are said to have crossed the Verecke Pass into the Carpathian Basin in 895 or 896, having lost their lands on the steppes of modern Ukraine to a Turkic tribe called the Pechenegs.)

The Avar empire of the previous century had been crushed by the Frankish forces of

Charlemagne. Slav tribes predominated for a while, but the instability in the region prevented their states (the Slovenian principality and the Moravian empire, for instance) from consolidating. So about 400,000 Hungarians may have arrived in the Carpathian Basin, to find a local population of about 200,000, which seems to have been rapidly absorbed.

The Hungarians, still pagan and illiterate at this time, rivaled the earlier Vikings in the way they raided and pillaged much of Europe over the next sixty years. The "arrows of the Hungarians" feature as a terrorist scenario in many early chronicles. So Europe breathed a collective sigh of relief when military defeats persuaded the Hungarian ruling prince, Géza, in about 970 to prepare his country for the feudal Christian monarchy that his son and successor, King Stephen, founded.

Medieval Kingdom

The kingdom of Hungary came into being at Christmas AD 1000, when Stephen I was crowned at Esztergom with a crown sent by Pope Sylvester II. Some people have interpreted the gift to mean that Stephen owed his crown to God, not Mammon—the Holy Roman Empire centered in modern Germany, which was the main power in Europe at the time. In fact, Sylvester and Emperor

Otto III were collaborating to consolidate Christianity and extend Christendom eastward in a political and religious sense. Stephen (István) was canonized in 1083.

By the time Stephen came to the throne, the Hungarians (Magyars) had been living in the Carpathian Basin for over a century and raiding in Europe for some time before that. Although medieval Hungary was almost completely devastated by Mongol incursions in 1241–2, it covered vast areas of central and southeastern Europe at various times. Buda became a center of the Renaissance under King Matthias I (1458–90), who amassed a famous library, second in size only to the Vatican's, and expanded the royal palace. Extensive remains of a summer palace can be seen at Visegrád.

Partition

The reversal was rapid. Hungary was disastrously defeated by the Ottoman Turks in the battle of Mohács in 1526, and the fleeing

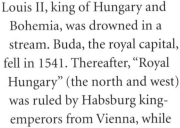

Louis II, king of Hungary and Bohemia, was drowned in a stream. Buda, the royal capital, fell in 1541. Thereafter, "Royal Hungary" (the north and west) was ruled by Habsburg king-emperors from Vienna, while

Central Hungary became a Turkish *sandjak* (province) under the pasha of Buda, and Transylvania a semi-independent principality—a haven of high cultural standards and religious toleration. Intermittent warfare between the Ottoman and Habsburg dominions continued.

Ottoman power in Hungary ended even more suddenly than it had begun. One moment Grand Vizir Kara Mustafa was boldly laying siege to Vienna in 1683, and the next he was suffering a succession of defeats. Buda was captured by Christian forces in 1686 and the Turks were ousted completely and irreversibly from Hungary by the 1699 Treaty of Karlowitz.

The legacy of the Ottoman period was mixed. The Turks had taxed the Hungarians hard, but they had left the towns to run their own affairs. Also, they had shown toleration toward Roman Catholicism, Protestantism, and Judaism, whereas the Habsburgs reimposed Catholicism by force.

The country was in a sorry, depopulated state in the late seventeenth century, but this was due as much to the warfare as to Ottoman misrule. There were few left to rejoice when Buda was captured. The combined Christian forces under Charles V, Duke of Lorraine, marked the occasion by sacking the city and conducting a pogrom against the Jews.

Modern Times

Nonetheless, Habsburg rule
allowed Hungary to begin
moving toward modern Europe.
There was a long but abortive
war of national independence
(1703–11) under Prince Ferenc

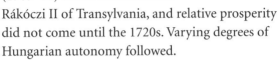

Rákóczi II of Transylvania, and relative prosperity
did not come until the 1720s. Varying degrees of
Hungarian autonomy followed.

Hungary, until the end of the First World War,
included modern Slovakia, Sub-Carpathian
Ukraine, Transylvania (now in Romania),
Vojvodina (now in Serbia), most of Croatia, and
the future Austrian province of Burgenland.
Agriculture benefited in the eighteenth century
from Imperial rule tempered by a Diet (legislative
assembly) of nobles, usually meeting in Pozsony
(Pressburg, modern Bratislava). But a truly
modern economy and society based on commerce,
industry, education, and toleration came later than
it did in Germany, Italy, or France.

Only in 1805 did officialdom begin to use
Hungarian alongside Latin, which survived as the
language spoken in the Diet until 1832. But
Hungarian development was unusual, as it was
led by the lower nobility and gentry, resentful of
aristocratic power, rather than by a bourgeoisie.
Acceleration of development in the 1830s and '40s

culminated in a bloodless revolution in Buda and Pest in March 1848, led by Lajos Kossuth. Inspired by similar events in Paris and Vienna, the reformists declared Hungary's autonomy within the Habsburg Empire. The subsequent war of independence was crushed by the Habsburgs the following year, with assistance from Tsarist Russia.

Many reforms were reversed, and harsh direct rule from Vienna continued for almost twenty years. Eventually, in 1867 the *Ausgleich*, or Compromise, brokered between the Hungarian nobility and the imperial court, created the Dual Austro-Hungarian Monarchy, in which Austria and Hungary had separate governments. This curious arrangement precipitated a forty-year spurt of belated bourgeois development—political, economic, and social development that set its mark on Budapest (created by a merger of Buda, Pest, and Óbuda in 1876) and made it the fastest-growing capital in Europe after Berlin.

Independence and Occupation

Hungary at last gained full independence after the First World War, but it lost 71 percent of its territory and 63 percent of its population under the 1920 Treaty of Trianon imposed at the Versailles peace conference. Sizeable Hungarian minorities are still found across the borders in Slovakia, Romania, and Serbia, as well as smaller communities in Ukraine, Croatia, Slovenia, and Austria.

After a 133-day Communist interlude in 1919, independent Hungary became a nominal kingdom again. It was headed from 1920 to 1944 by a regent, Miklós Horthy, previously a rear admiral in the Austro-Hungarian navy, although Charles IV of Habsburg made two attempts to regain his throne in 1921. One candidate for king considered by royalists was the British press baron Lord Rothermere, whose *Daily Mail* published articles in 1927 calling for revision of the terms of the Trianon treaty.

But Horthy remained. He and successive conservative, irredentist governments he appointed aligned the country with Italy and Germany, in return for what turned out to be very temporary territorial gains in the late 1930s and early 1940s. Rampant anti-Semitism came after German military occupation in March 1944, followed by a German-engineered coup d'état in October. Some 600,000 Hungarian Jews were sent to death camps, along with large numbers of Gypsies.

The Soviet army that defeated the German and Hungarian forces in 1944–5 was ill-disciplined, and the reprisals were severe. Huge reparations had to be paid. About half a million Hungarians were deported to labor camps in the Soviet Union, from which many never returned. Initially, Hungary had its own democratic government alongside a Soviet-dominated Allied Control Commission, but the Communists undermined it, gaining power without an armed conflict in 1948 and imposing a classic Communist regime.

Stalinist rule under the local dictator Mátyás Rákosi brought oppression, upheaval, and impossible economic strains. Faced with the imminent collapse of its satellite state, Khrushchev's Russia in 1953 supported the installation of a reformist government under Imre Nagy, but then the Kremlin vacillated, allowing Rákosi to return. This led during 1956 to mounting protest and finally rebellion.

The '56 Revolution

The sight of Soviet tanks firing into crowds in a Communist satellite country shook the world in October 1956. If the Suez Crisis and the invasion of Egypt hadn't distracted the world's attention from Hungary, there might conceivably have been

United Nations intervention, as the Hungarian revolutionaries were hoping.

The '56 Revolution was by no means the only revolution in Hungarian history, but it's the one whose scars remain in some Budapest streets, and the one to influence many events during and since the fall of the Communist regime in 1989–90.

Mátyás Rákosi retrieved power in the spring of 1955 from Prime Minister Imre Nagy, a cautious reformer whom the Soviet leadership under Nikita Khrushchev had supported for a while. But Rákosi's orthodox Communist policies had clearly failed by the summer of 1956. The standard of living was far short of what it had been in 1941, when Hungary entered the Second World War. Proletarian rule simply meant dictatorship. The secret police were ubiquitous, although the worst repression was over by then. Rákosi was ousted a second time, and his successor, Ernő Gerő, promised changes, but did nothing.

By that time, ideas for reform were being openly discussed and becoming increasingly radical, but the uprising, when it came, was sudden and unforeseen. On October 22, a student rally at Budapest Technical University listed sixteen demands, including free elections, withdrawal of Soviet troops, and higher pay. There was unrest in Poland as well.

On October 23, a student march was joined spontaneously by workers and employees. By evening, 200,000 people were standing before Parliament, as a crowd elsewhere in the city toppled the giant statue of Stalin, and another crowd outside the Radio was calling angrily for the Sixteen Points to be broadcast. The Hungarian party leadership appointed Imre Nagy to head a new government. The Radio was stormed, and the first Soviet troops to enter the capital the next morning met armed resistance. Most units of the Hungarian army stood aside, while many officers and men went over to the freedom fighters.

By October 26, there was a general strike. Revolutionary councils in communities and factories were in control, demanding Soviet withdrawal and a neutral, democratic, independent  Hungary. The revolution spread to other cities, where Soviet units were confronted by rebels, and Hungarian army units stood aside.

Initially concerned to appease the Soviets, the Western Powers plucked up courage on October 27 and called on the UN Security Council to debate the situation. On the night of October 27–8, a ceasefire was brokered, Soviet troops withdrew from Budapest, and negotiations started on Soviet withdrawal. But this Communist-brokered deal foundered, partly because the revolutionaries refused to disarm or go back to work.

A Soviet decision to crush the uprising and replace the reformist government was made in Moscow on the night of October 30–31 and carried out on November 4. The Nagy government took refuge in the Yugoslav 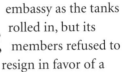 embassy as the tanks rolled in, but its members refused to resign in favor of a puppet regime under János Kádár, which was sworn in on November 7.

Sporadic fighting continued until November 11, and political and civil resistance into the New Year. The UN General Assembly confined itself to condemning the Soviet aggression.

Kádár made initial concessions and promised an amnesty, but over the next three years, the Communist reprisals and terror led to 13,000 people being interned, over 20,000 imprisoned, and some 230 executed, Nagy and other senior figures among them. Most prisoners were released in a 1963 amnesty, but several were held until the mid-1970s. Many were never allowed to work in their original occupations again.

About 180,000 Hungarians, the majority young and male, fled into exile. They included, for instance, almost the whole Hungarian Olympic team in Melbourne, Australia, and all the staff and students of the forestry faculty at Sopron College, who stayed together and completed their degree courses in British Columbia.

Reprisals and Reforms
Perhaps it is not too fanciful to draw parallels between the long Kádár period (1956–89) and the period of direct Habsburg rule (1849–67). Both were initially brutal. Both were absolutist, though in some degree enlightened. Each rested on a small elite of questionable legitimacy or suitability for running a modern state.

Kádár's Communist Hungary tinkered with the Soviet model and sought to promote economic and political détente with the West. The reforms it introduced culminated in a voluntary abdication of power in 1989–90.

Communism had been costly to maintain, and what with the high price of conversion to capitalism, Hungary had foreign debts that peaked in 1995 at 84 percent of the annual economic output (GDP).

Some longer-term social effects of the Communist period are discussed in Chapter 2.

Change of System
The collapse of Communism and transformation of a Soviet satellite country into an independent parliamentary democracy with a fast-growing

market economy is known in Hungary as the "change of system" *(rendszerváltás).*

Hungary passed the big tests in the economic and political spheres. Economically, it went for a gradual approach, rather than the sudden "shock therapy" preferred in several other post-Communist countries, where most of the state assets were given away to the public.

Successive Hungarian governments have put great efforts into establishing the institutions and rule of law essential if a modern economy is to thrive, if not always with complete success. But the price has been a yawning gap between rich and poor; intermittent public nostalgia for the safer, stagnant society of old; obscene profits made by banks and others exploiting the imperfections of the market; and more.

Eleven centuries after arriving in Central Europe, the Hungarians acceded to the European Union, on May 1, 2004. But the path from one entry to the other had not been smooth.

GOVERNMENT

Hungary is a republic—a parliamentary democracy with a nonexecutive head of state, so that executive power is in the hands of the government, headed by the prime minister. Hungary's constitution dates from 1948 and was modeled on the Soviet one, but it was radically altered in 1989, so that it now bears little resemblance to the original document. Parliament (officially the National Assembly) has a single chamber with members elected by all citizens over the age of eighteen except for those specifically barred from doing so, such as criminals.

The complex election system adopted after the Communist period was modeled on Germany's. There are up to 210 seats to be won by proportional representation from twenty regions, and a possible 58 seats to be filled from national party lists. MPs are also chosen on a constituency basis. Parties must win 5 percent of the aggregate list votes to qualify for any list seats in Parliament at all. Each voter has two votes in the first round, one for a regional list and the other for a constituency member. Almost half the members are elected from constituencies by a direct majority, usually after two rounds of voting.

The head of state is the president of the republic, who is elected for a five-year term by a two-thirds majority of Parliament. The president has to sign all parliamentary legislation and has limited powers to delay it, refer it back for reconsideration, or submit it to the Constitutional Court. He (at present) also has powers to initiate legislation and issue judicial pardons. The president resides and works in a modest palace on Castle Hill. The extensive Prime

Minister's Office, a kind of super-ministry, is housed partly in the Parliament building.

Parliament elects the prime minister by a simple majority and has to approve his government. (There has not been a female prime minister so far) General elections are held regularly every four years and by-elections for vacant parliamentary seats once a year. At present, local elections are held in the first year of each new government term. Some foreigners also qualify to vote in local and European elections as residents or as E.U. citizens.

POLITICS

The first free general elections in 1990 resulted in a relatively right-wing coalition. Each of the three general elections thereafter—in 1994, 1998, and 2002—turned out an incumbent government. This ability to change governments peacefully is seen by political scientists as an important test of the viability of a new democracy.

However, relations are extremely bad between the present governing parties (the Socialists and the small Alliance of Free Democrats) and the more right-wing opposition parties (FIDESZ and the small Hungarian Democratic Forum).

Each general election so far has been followed by widespread dismissals of officials and functionaries, as the new government maneuvers its own people into crucial or lucrative positions. Parliament is often sparsely attended, and dogged by ill temper and insults. Cooperation between the government and the opposition is minimal. Libel suits involving politicians are frequent and protracted. These aspects tend to erode the overall public reputation of politics and politicians.

On the other hand, turnouts in general elections have been improving steadily, from 65 percent in the first round and 46 percent in the second in 1990, to 71 and 74 percent respectively in 2002. This too is probably explained by the increasing left/right polarization of the parties and acrimony among them.

Parliament elects, with a two-thirds majority, the eleven members of the Constitutional Court, who sit for nine-year terms and rule on whether legislation is constitutional or not. It has proved extremely difficult to find nonpartisan candidates in the present political climate.

Similar problems arise with electing ombudsmen, the head of the national audit authority, the chief prosecutor, and the chief justice. By and large, the Constitutional Court and the judiciary generally are well trusted, but there have been periodic attacks on the audit authority and the prosecution service. Respect for politicians seems to be at an all-time low, although such loss of prestige is not peculiar to Hungary.

ECONOMIC TRANSFORMATION

The Hungarian economy has successfully transformed itself over the last fifteen years. When Communism collapsed in 1989–90, it was still a "state-socialist" economy in which the state owned or controlled almost the entire economy.

Privatization, mainly in the 1990s, has left Hungary with a higher proportion of private ownership than some Western European countries. Foreign ownership of the economy is also high.

The initial result was deep recession, but growth speeded up after 1995, aided by budgetary conservatism and high foreign investment in advance of full E.U. membership, which was achieved in 2004. However, growth has been slowing and budget discipline becoming more lax in the last five years. (The economy is treated in more detail in Chapter 8.)

BUDAPEST

The capital of Hungary dominates the country far more thoroughly than Vienna dominates Austria or London dominates the United Kingdom. For a start, look at a map of Hungary. All the main roads and railways radiate from Budapest. Today, Hungary is busy, rather belatedly, building itself some express highways—and how will they run? Out from Budapest in all directions, just like the roads and railways before them.

One can demonstrate this dominance in economic terms. Budapest, where 17 percent of Hungary's population live and/or work, accounts for 33 percent of its economic output (GDP). About 35 percent of the country's university and college students study in Budapest. And more than 99 percent of the air passengers and air cargo entering Hungary land at Budapest Ferihegy Airport.

This dominance is nothing new. Extensive remains of a Roman camp and civilian town of Aquincum can still be seen in Óbuda, the city's 3rd District. Aquincum became administrative capital of the Roman province of Pannonia Inferior (parts of Western Hungary and Slovakia) in AD 108 and remained important until the barbarian invasions of the early fifth century.

The Castle of Buda *(Budavár)*, overlooking Óbuda, was the royal seat and capital of Hungary for most of the Middle Ages, although some kings based themselves at Esztergom, Székesfehérvár, or Visegrád. Central Hungary under the Ottoman Empire was controlled by the pasha of Buda, while the Habsburg regions of the divided country were ruled from Pozsony (Bratislava, capital of Slovakia) and the Transylvanian princes held court at Kolozsvár (today's Cluj-Napoca in Romania). Pozsony remained the usual place for the assembly of nobles to meet, but its slim pretensions to be a capital ended in 1848.

By that time, Pest and Buda, on the left and right banks of the Danube respectively, made up the country's main urban area, but Hungary was still dominated by the countryside and agriculture, not its towns. Rapid development of the capital began after the *Ausgleich* of 1867 and the union of Pest, Buda, and Óbuda as Budapest in 1876. By the end of the century, Budapest had 717,681 inhabitants.

Hungary's territorial losses after the First World War accentuated the dominance of Budapest. Such cities as Pozsony (Bratislava) and Kassa (Košice) were ceded to Czechoslovakia, Kolozsvár (Cluj-Napoca), Nagyvárad (Oradea), Brassó (Preşov), and Temesvár (Timişoara) to Romania, and Újvidék (Novi Sad) to the new Yugoslav kingdom. Several surrounding towns and villages were merged into Budapest in 1948, creating a city of 1.6 million inhabitants.

Budapest today has a population of just below 1.7 million, whereas the next-largest city, Debrecen, has only 200,000 inhabitants.

The capital city is run by its municipality under an elected chief mayor and a sixty-seven-member assembly, which appoints a chief clerk. However, the city is divided into twenty-three districts, each of which has a similar structure of mayor and assembly. An uneasy, rather arbitrary division of labor has emerged between the municipality and the district governments.

The Danube, here 1,000–2,000 feet (300–600 meters) wide, runs between the steep hills of Buda and the plains of Pest. The views are stunning from both sides, as many of the city's main buildings can be seen from the banks— Parliament, the Royal Palace of Buda, and the Buda Castle District, the towers and domes of the main churches, the Academy of Sciences, the Gresham Palace, and other great nineteenth-century buildings. This is a UNESCO World Heritage site.

Moving downstream from north to south, the first main island in Budapest is Hajógyár (Shipyard) Island off Óbuda, scene of the congenial Sziget (Island) rock festival every summer. Traffic-free Margaret Island is the city's most attractive and popular public park, with swimming pools and a couple of hotels. Csepel Island, in the south of the city, accommodates the industrial 21st District of Budapest, as well as several other towns and villages.

"NO HARD FEELINGS"

The name of Hungary's ambassador to the European Union has a familiar ring. Dr. György Habsburg, born in 1961, is the grandson of Hungary's last king, Charles IV. He was also elected president of the Hungarian Red Cross in 2004. This is surprising, because members of the Habsburg dynasty were seldom popular during the 450 years when Hungary, or much of it, was part of their empire.

One exception was Queen Elizabeth (Sissi), consort of Emperor-King Francis Joseph, who has a Budapest bridge named after her. She was a "Diana"—adored in Hungary from the belated coronation in 1867 until her assassination in 1898. The *Sissi* trilogy of films (1955–7) starring Romy Schneider is essential viewing for Central Europe buffs.

Francis Joseph's great-nephew Charles IV (Charles I to the Austrians) was less lucky. He came to the throne in 1916 but his empire fell apart two years later. Bungled attempts at a separate peace with the Allies and two comic-opera attempted coups in Hungary in 1920 did nothing for his reputation. He died in exile in Madeira in 1922. Pope John Paul II made a baffling decision to beatify him in 2003.

The one to restore the Habsburgs to Hungarian favor was Charles's son and György's father. Born in 1912 and christened Franz Josef Otto Robert Maria Anton Karl Max Heinrich Sixtus Xavier Felix René Ludwig Gaetano Pius Ignazius, Otto von Habsburg (Habsburg Ottó in Hungarian) is a genial, garrulous, energetic man. He renounced claims to the Hungarian throne in 1961. As a member of the European Parliament until 1999 and president of the Pan-European Movement, he campaigned fervently for Hungary's membership in the European Union. He speaks Hungarian with an engaging German accent.

There were moves to nominate Otto von Habsburg for the presidency of Hungary in 1990, but he apparently declined to run.

Some Key Dates

35 BCE–433 CE Roman rule over Pannonia.

895–6 The Magyars began to settle in the Carpathian Basin, and made raids throughout Europe until 970. Transylvania colonized.

972–97 Prince Géza sent envoys to the Holy Roman Emperor and accepted Christian missionaries in Hungary.

1000–1038 Stephen (István) I, as first king, established a Western Christian feudal state.

1083 Stephen I, his son Emericus (Imre), and his evangelist, Bishop Gerard (Gellért), canonized.

1172–96 The reign of Béla III, under whom Hungary became a major power in the Balkans.

1192–5 The Pray Codex contained the "Funeral Oration," the earliest continuous Hungarian text.

1241–2 Hungary sacked by Mongol hordes.

1301 The royal House of Árpád died out with Andrew III. He was succeeded after six years' civil war by Charles (Károly) I of Anjou.

1342–82 Louis (Lajos) I conquered Dalmatia. He expelled the Jews from Hungary in 1360. He became king of Poland as well in 1370.

1433 Sigismund (Zsigmond) of Luxemburg, King of Hungary (since 1387, Bohemia since 1420, and Milan since 1431), crowned Holy Roman Emperor.

1456 Governor János Hunyadi defended Belgrade against the Ottoman Turks, halting their advance.

1458–90 King Matthias (Mátyás) I Corvinus centralized government. Hungary became a strong military power and cultural center.

1526 The battle of Mohács. Under Sulaiman the Magnificent the Turks defeated the Hungarians.

1541 Buda captured by the Turks.

1570 The Treaty of Speyer partitioned Hungary between the Ottoman and Habsburg empires, with Transylvania as a separate independent principality. Intermittent warfare continued.

1672 Rebellion against the Habsburgs escalated under Imre Thököly, who founded a Turkish-allied principality in north Hungary in 1678.

1686 Buda sacked after its recapture from the Turks by Christian forces. Thököly crushed.

1699 Hungary freed from the Turks by the Peace of Karlowitz, and reunited under Habsburg rule.

1703–11 Prince Ferenc Rákóczi II led a Hungarian uprising against Austria, forcing it to promise to respect the Hungarian constitution.

1722 The Pragmatic Sanction agreed upon between the Diet and the Habsburgs governed Hungary's constitutional relations to its kings.

1777 The *ratio educationis* law left the Churches to run the schools.

1809 Napoleon advanced from Vienna to Győr. The Hungarian *insurrectio*, or noble militia, was called out for the last time and lost the battle.

1825 Count István Széchenyi funded a Scholarly Society, forerunner of the Hungarian Academy of Sciences. Development in the Age of Reform.

1844 Hungarian became the official language, but less than half the population were Hungarian.

1848 European unrest spread to Pest. Lajos Kossuth took the lead in the national revolution. The semifeudal Diet gave way to a National Assembly. War broke out, but the Croats and others sided with Vienna.

1849 The National Assembly repudiated the Habsburgs and elected Kossuth head of state. Russia intervened and Hungary surrendered. Executions and direct rule ensued. Kossuth in exile promoted Hungary as an archetype of an oppressed nation.

1867 The *Ausgleich* (compromise) with the Habsburgs gave Hungary self-government, and equality with Austria within a dual monarchy. Economic and social development followed.

1868 The Education Act provided for six years of compulsory schooling in the local language, with state supervision. Emancipation of the Jews.

1914 Austria-Hungary declared war on Serbia, precipitating the First World War.

1918–19 Defeated, the Habsburg Empire broke up. A revolution on October 30, 1918, led by Count Mihály Károlyi, foundered over imposed territorial losses. A second revolution on March 21, 1919, installed a Communist regime under Béla Kun, but Czech and Romanian forces attacked and an army under Admiral Miklós Horthy seized power. Reprisals followed.

1920 Parliament elected Horthy regent. The *numerus clausus* law restricted the proportion of Jews in higher education and some professions. The Treaty of Trianon confirmed that Hungary could retain only 29 percent of its former territory with 37 percent of its population.

1932–6 Foreign policy under the Gömbös government swung Hungary behind the German–Italian Axis.

1938 The first Jewish law restricted Jewish employment. The Hitler-brokered First Vienna Award ceded parts of Slovakia to Hungary.

1939 Subcarpathia (the Czechoslovak province of Ruthenia) ceded to Hungary. The second Jewish law defined Jews in racial terms, restricted political rights of Jews, curbed employment further, and introduced labor service for "unreliable elements."

1940 The Second Vienna Award ceded north Transylvania to Hungary.

1941 Hungary joined the German attack on Yugoslavia and was rewarded with territory lost in 1920. War with the Soviet Union and Britain.

1943 The Hungarian Second Army annihilated at the Don Bend.

1944 German occupation installed a Nazi regime. Horthy failed to bail Hungary out of the war and resigned. Jewish deportation to death camps began. An interim legislature met in the Soviet-held city of Debrecen.

1945 Armistice. The Soviets expelled the last German forces. Hungary had lost a million people and 40 percent of its national wealth in the Second World War. Free general elections held.

1946 Communist influence steadily increased, helped by the Soviet-run Allied Control Commission. Currency reform.

1946–8 Nationalization of the economy and education. The 1920 frontiers restored by treaty.

1948 A forced merger of the Communist and Social Democratic parties brought Soviet-style one-party dictatorship under Mátyás Rákosi. Living standards plummeted as resources diverted to heavy industry. Mass internment and relocation. Cardinal Mindszenty, head of the Catholic Church, among many show-trial victims.

1955 Reform-minded Communist Imre Nagy dismissed as prime minister. Hungary and the other Soviet satellites concluded the Warsaw Pact.

1956 Anti-Soviet uprising broke out in Budapest. Imre Nagy, recalled as prime minister, announced Hungary's withdrawal from the Warsaw Pact. Hopes of Western or UN assistance faded and Soviet forces returned to the capital, installing a quisling government under János Kádár.

1956–8 Brutal reprisals brought more than 200 executions, including those of Imre Nagy.

1959 Collectivization of agriculture completed.

1968 A New Economic Mechanism of "market socialism" introduced. Hungary assisted in the Soviet occupation of Czechoslovakia.

1978 The U.S.A. under President Jimmy Carter returned the Holy Crown and coronation regalia sent there after the Second World War.

1984 A visit by British Prime Minister Margaret Thatcher confirmed relations with the West.

1987–8 Opposition groups formed openly. János Kádár dropped as head of the Communist Party.

1989 Roundtable Communist–opposition talks charted a course to multiparty democracy. János Kádár died. U.S. President George Bush visited. Hungary opened its border with Austria for East German refugees to flee to the West, so breaching the Iron Curtain. A new republic was declared.

1990 Soviet occupation forces withdrew. Elections produced a center-right coalition government that pursued radical free-market reforms.

1990–2000 A market economy was restored and mass privatization of state assets occurred.

1994 Hungary applied to join the E.U. General elections produced a socialist-liberal coalition.

1995 Hungary joined the Organization for Economic Cooperation and Development (OECD). Visitors included U.S. President Bill Clinton and Pope John Paul II.

1998 General elections brought a right-wing coalition.

1999 Hungary joined NATO and made facilities available for bombing Serbia. It later gave assistance to the U.S. in Afghanistan and Iraq.

2002 General elections led to a socialist-liberal coalition.

2004 Hungary joined the E.U.

chapter two

VALUES & ATTITUDES

Hungary has had a stroke of luck. Unlike many other countries and peoples, it has an image in the outside world that it can live with—or even play up to. Though some parts of that image seem random or even misplaced, many have embedded themselves as virtues to be cultivated and displayed. But behind them lie other values and attitudes that visiting tourists, businesspeople, or journalists are less likely to know in advance.

IMAGE AND SELF-IMAGE

Just as there's brave little Belgium in Western Europe, so there's brave little Hungary in Central Europe. (Central Europe, with its cultural echoes of *Mitteleuropa*, is seen as preferable as a designation to Eastern Europe, with its overtones of the drab Soviet period.) Hungarians earned that reputation as a brave, beleaguered

people in sixteenth- to nineteenth-century wars against the Ottoman and Habsburg empires. It was regained in the twentieth century, through the 1945–90 Soviet occupation, and especially the defiance shown in the 1956 Revolution.

But there are other, deep, Hungarian historical grievances. The deepest is the Treaty of Trianon, which truncated the country after the First World War. Such resentments are perplexing and even distasteful to outsiders, rather as Irish national grievances can seem to British people. But just as few Irishmen aspire to let off bombs in Belfast these days, so few Hungarians seriously contemplate revising the country's Trianon borders. There are no territorial claims, yet the grievance lives on, as part of a feeling of national melancholy. The Hungarians still feel bloodied but unbowed.

At this point, it must be said that Hungary has a different image in Central and Eastern Europe from the one it has in the rest of the world. Just as Hungarians are often resentful of neighboring countries, so neighboring peoples are often resentful of Hungary, and of the Hungarian minority communities in their midst. That applies to varying degrees, of course: more strongly in Slovakia and Romania, hardly at all in Austria or Slovenia.

One difference between the two images of Hungary is in the degree of familiarity they reflect. According to a Hungarian Tourist Office international survey, some 15 percent of Poles, for instance, who traveled abroad in 1998–2002 went to Hungary, but only 2 percent of British travelers did. In both countries, those who had never been to Hungary knew scarcely anything about it. Both British and Italian visitors in that period made frequent mention in their survey responses of "pleasant surprise" at not being overwhelmed by Eastern bloc grayness or poverty.

CULTURE

While neighboring Central European peoples often see nationalism as a Hungarian characteristic and a potential threat, those Western Europeans and North Americans who have an image of Hungarians at all are likely to see them as cultured, hospitable, vivacious, and resourceful. Now there's an image worth living up to, as many Hungarians realize.

Factors behind the "cultured" perception must include the contribution that Hungarians like Alexander Korda and George Cukor made to the film industry between the 1930s and the 1960s, and Hungarian composers such as Liszt, Kálmán, Lehár, Dohnányi, Bartók, and Kodály, and the conductor Sir Georg Solti, made to world music in the nineteenth and twentieth centuries.

But are Hungarians more cultured or educated than most? It's safe to say that Hungarian gymnasia (academically oriented secondary schools) make greater demands on their students than English comprehensives or American high schools do. Family expectations of middle-class children are higher too. As an illustration of what the gymnasium system has been able to do, look at the fifteen Nobel prizewinners who were born and at least partly educated in Hungary—twice as many as Germany, relative to the population.

Not that all teenagers go to gymnasia. Many of the vocational secondary schools provide a low standard of general education alongside dubious or obsolete vocational skills. Nonetheless, a recent international survey of the math skills of seventh-year schoolchildren put Hungary in twelfth place in the world. (The U.K. came twenty-fourth and the U.S.A. twenty-second.)

THE AFTERMATH OF COMMUNISM
More than fifteen years have gone by since Hungary emerged in 1989–90 from forty years of totalitarian Communist rule. Those four decades have left strong marks on how Hungarians relate to each other and how they see themselves.

The Communist regime, headed after 1956 by
János Kádár, built up a stock of goodwill in the
West in the 1970s and 1980s, with a more jovial,
consumerist brand of "Frigidaire socialism." It
ran its economy rather differently than Russia's,
so that there wouldn't be breadlines. Hungary
was seen as the Soviet satellite prepared to sail
closest to the wind with its initiatives to improve
East–West relations—as the Soviet Union's
stalking horse, of course. And the Kádár regime
liked to present an avant-garde image in the
arts as well.

Fears and Chances
Kádár and his handpicked elite presented
themselves as benevolent tacticians, allowing the
Hungarians to get away with as much as possible
without upsetting their masters in Moscow. Fear
of Moscow was one factor, certainly, but there was
another: fear of their own people. Nobody would
want another bloody, bitter '56 Revolution, would
they? Even when taken at face value, that
perception of Hungary's role in world politics
suggested a measure of cynicism. Hungary's
Communists weren't as Communist as all that.

They weren't indeed. Hungary's well-placed
Communists were gratified to find they could
act as a political and economic elite that did
very well for itself, and if the price was lip

service to Communism, so be it. Many Hungarians today suspect that members of the same ex-Communist elite did very well later, too, out of post-Communist privatization.

But the Communist system, even in its superficially humanized, marketized Hungarian version, was the most extensively totalitarian system the world had ever known. Nazism and fascism might have outdone Communism in savagery, but the Communist system won on breadth and comprehensiveness. It did not just cover government and local government, the organizations of society and politics, the armed forces, and the education system, as fascism did. It annihilated or annexed *all* civil initiative and held *absolute* sway over the economy.

That applied also in Hungary, even if Kádár's regime toyed with the idea of granting freedom of action to some members of the Communist elite—in their guise as company managers—to respond to limited, distorted market forces, if they felt so inclined. If they didn't feel so inclined, they could join the crowd of other managers of state-owned "enterprises," as the corporations were called, pleading for special treatment and extra state funds. There was little risk involved. Just one major firm (in the construction industry) was allowed to go bust under the Kádár regime.

All the other loss makers were bailed out, time and time again.

SOCIAL FRAGMENTATION

That total Communist control caused society to fragment into tiny units that gained huge significance for the people they comprised. Ties of family and friendship, old classmates and teachers, neighbors and acquaintances became the stuff of society, because the normal tiers of civil society found in Western countries had been destroyed. Dependence on personal ties has remained in the post-Communist era since 1990. How this affects foreigners in Hungary today is discussed in Chapters 4 and 8.

Another legacy of the Communist period is low inclination to save money. For all its faults, the Communist system provided a welfare state (on huge foreign loans!): free medical care; pensions based on right, not lifetime contributions; sick pay; the right to work; child care allowances; and subsidized cafeteria meals, food, clothing, housing, education, transportation, theater, books, recordings, and vacations, for example. Wages, on the other hand, were meager and showed little differentiation according to effort.

Productivity was low: "You pretend to pay us and we pretend to work," was the joke at the time.

And the heavy welfare spending was poorly matched with needs. Take public housing as an example. It was allocated according to a composite of criteria, of which "need" was only one. Often apartments were allocated to friends and relations of people with influence in the housing department.

Effectively, there was discrimination *against* the proletariat in what was supposed to be a proletarian state. Officials, clerical workers, and supervisors—hard to describe as working class at all—had a good chance of being allocated an apartment, but lower-ranking workers received, if they were lucky, a cheap plot of land on which to build their own home in their spare time.

The luckier, better-placed Communist-Party comrades had not only obtained some scarce public housing ready-made, but they paid very low rent for it. Here was a situation of chronic housing shortage, with a great deal of government money being spent on subsidizing the rents of some of the people who least needed it.

SPENDING

There was little incentive to save in those days. Often the problem was to find something sensible to buy with the money you had. Many people did better by throwing parties for the rich and influential than they would have done by putting their money in the bank, as bank deposits shrank before one's eyes, earning negative real interest. Others built themselves marble bathrooms or enjoyed vacations abroad—Hungary, unlike most Soviet-bloc countries, allowed foreign travel to many citizens after 1964.

The high inflation of the 1990s did nothing to persuade people to be thrifty either. Even today, the first investment choice for most families is property—spending on the home, or a second home, or a child's home, or a grandmother's home that will be inherited one day.

In a 2005 international survey, 72 percent of the Hungarian respondents said they didn't save money at all, as compared with 43 percent of Americans and 23 percent of Western Europeans.

PATRIOTISM

Hungarians have a strong sense of nationhood. But this loyalty to the "nation" means two or even three things at once.

Hungarians are loyal to their country and fellow citizens, regardless of social or ethnic affiliation. In other words, they are patriotic in the way that Americans are patriotic. There is no British-style embarrassment about flying the

flag or standing up to sing
fervently the Hungarians'
stirring, haunting national
anthem, "God Bless the
Hungarians." (*Isten, áldd-
meg a' Magyart,* written by
Ferenc Kölcsey in 1823, published in 1828, set to
music by Ferenc Erkel in 1844, but not adopted as
the official anthem until 1903. You can read it and
hear it on http://ingeb.org/songs/istenald.html.)

Hungarians identify with their linguistic
community: the thirteen or fourteen million
people in Hungary, Romania, Slovakia, Ukraine,
Serbia, Croatia, Slovenia, and Austria whose
native language is Hungarian. Most of these live
in areas that belonged to the Kingdom of
Hungary before the First World War.

Some people go on to identify a Hungarian
cultural or even ethnic community to which they
belong, and draw unsavory sociopolitical
conclusions from that. The nation in this sense is
seen as something positive, but monolithic,
burdened, not enriched by its minorities or
possessors of parallel identities. Most of the small
linguistic minorities of present-day Hungary
(Germans, Romanians, Slovaks, and other Slavs)
have effectively been assimilated. The issue is seen at
its most acute in relation to the Roma communities.

ATTITUDES TOWARD THE ROMA

Altogether 404,760 Hungarians—4 percent of the population—declared themselves to be Roma in the 2000 national census. Many others refrained from doing so as a reaction to widespread racial prejudice. (The term *cigány*, the Hungarian for Gypsy, is coming to be seen as derogatory. The "weasel word" is *kisebbségi*—minority.)

Roma can usually be distinguished from other Hungarians. They tend to have darker skin, and their accents, clothes, customs, and body language are distinctive, at least to other Hungarians.

The highest proportions of Roma (7–10 percent of the population) are found in the relatively deprived northeast of the country and in Budapest. There are three subdivisions of the Roma: the "Hungarian" or "musical" Roma (all Hungarian speaking, the most integrated of the three), the Wallachian Roma (who may speak a Romany language known to linguists as Vlach Lovar), and the Beás Roma (who may still speak an archaic dialect of Romanian).

Over half the sample in some surveys of Hungarian public opinion state negative opinions of "Gypsies"—dishonest, lazy, dirty, and so on. This contrasts with 5–10 percent expressing prejudice against the Jews, for example.

"The Roma are the real losers by the change of system," as Gábor Kertesi, a Hungarian authority, writes at the beginning of his recent study of Roma employment and education: "They lost their traditional crafts and economic functions in the first half of the twentieth century, and now they have lost the unskilled jobs in metal-bashing industries that they gained during the acute labor shortages of the Communist period."

The social disadvantage of Hungarian Roma appears in their social structure, employment, skills, education, housing, and state of health.

Roma are far behind the general population in the amount of schooling they manage to complete. To give one comparison, 49 percent of all Hungarian students who complete the eight compulsory grades of elementary education go on to a four-year course of secondary schooling that leads to a certificate of secondary education *(érettségi)*. The proportion among Hungarian Roma students is 3 percent. The social facts leave the majority of Hungary's Roma as an underclass, heavily dependent on welfare benefits and making little progress toward integration into the majority society or the economy.

ATTITUDES TOWARD AUTHORITY
Hungarians, by and large, are keen on law and order, but they haven't had entirely positive experiences with those who are supposed to keep it. At least not in the last eighty years or so.

Police, the secret services, and the Communist militia (the last now abolished) all came under the Ministry of the Interior in the Communist period and formed a state within a state, especially the network of informers in all walks of life and the agents controlling them. Their crimes are presented graphically at the House of Terror (*Terror Háza*, VI. Andrássy út 60.)

Military conscription, by the way, was abolished as of November 3, 2004, when the last batch of Hungarians ended their compulsory military service. The move to professional armed forces brought Hungary into line with almost all E.U. countries.

MEN AND WOMEN

Relations between men and women in Hungary may strike people from English-speaking countries as old-fashioned. Most couples seem to divide their responsibilities in a traditional way. Women cook, shop, and clean, while men look after money matters and the DIY, and do outdoor tasks such as mowing, digging, or car washing. Men may have become more involved in child rearing in recent decades but, as in the rest of Europe, there are fewer children to rear.

The courtesies due to women are obvious and the feminism of

Hungarian women seldom extends to resenting these. A woman goes out of a room or into an elevator first. The man usually drives, pushes the stroller, and carries the bags. In the street, the man traditionally walks on the woman's left— apparently because of how swords were worn. Women are served before men in a restaurant. The bill will be brought to the man, and the woman will be helped on with her coat.

Even in the workplace, many of these courtesies are still observed. It's customary to compliment a woman on a new hairdo, and on her clothes from time to time. On the darker side, flirtation bordering on harassment can occur with young women at work, despite the Hungarian saying, "Don't shoot your tame rabbit."

Fathers and Lovers

Hungarian men are demonstrative suitors, and to hear them talk, and watch them bow, smirk, and present bunches of flowers, you'd think you were in France or Italy. They also like to talk about their conquests; but before you lock up your daughters and threaten your spouse, consider whether they might not be exaggerating in this respect. A few reasons follow.

Extramarital relationships cost time and money, and few Hungarians have much of either.

Social life is centered on a circle of extended

family and old friends. Hungarians do less business travel and have less time for fishing trips than their counterparts in English-speaking countries, making peccadilloes harder to hide.

Hungarians go to bed early. If, as the Hungarian writer George Mikes remarked in *How to Be an Alien*, "Continental people have sex life; the English have hot-water bottles," the Hungarians have second jobs, weight problems, a tendency to fall asleep in front of the television, unreliable cars, children to attend to, nosy parents and siblings, politics to argue about, gardens to tend . . .

Although the divorce rate is high, the cause is as likely to be estrangement, unacceptable behavior, violence, or drinking as infidelity. Even in cases of infidelity, spouses are likely to turn a blind eye or patch up their differences. Separation and divorce are expensive.

CHURCHGOING

According to the 2001 census, 55 percent of Hungarians are Roman Catholic (and another 3 percent Greek Catholic), 15 percent Reformed Protestant, 3 percent Evangelical (Lutheran), and under 1 percent religious Jews, while 15 percent say they have no religious affiliation.

Self-description is not a good guide to religious

fervor, so this is statistically uncertain ground. But surveys suggest that 21 percent of Hungarians were attending an act of worship once a week in 1991; in 1996–7, 15 percent called themselves religiously active, and 55 percent said they practiced religion "in their own way."

Here Hungarian values and attitudes conform to those of Western Europe, rather than North America. Although the contentious estimates of "regular church attendance" in the U.S.A. vary between 26 and 42 percent and the proportion in Hungary's neighbor Austria is about 30 percent, in the U.K. it is about 10 percent and in Sweden only 6 percent. The figures for Hungary cast doubt on how far the religious decline can be blamed on the Communist regime as such, as they are in line with the tendencies in much of Europe.

Despite the fact that the dominant Catholic Church outlaws contraception, not to mention abortion and divorce, the birthrate is 9.4 per thousand and falling. There are over 55,000 abortions a year among a population of 2,200,000 women between the ages of fifteen and forty-four. Also, there are fifty divorces in Hungary for every one hundred marriages.

Christian teaching lost much ground under Communist rule. The official doctrines of atheistic materialism and supremacy of the state over the individual were taught in schools and reflected in the media, where any belief in God was scorned. Religious orders were banned, churchmen (including, as we have seen, Cardinal József Mindszenty, head of the Catholic Church) were imprisoned, religious schools were closed, and religious activity was confined to church premises. Religious affiliations were incompatible with Communist-Party membership, so churchgoers were in practice excluded from almost all positions of responsibility.

Toleration increased in the 1960s, but it came with stronger attempts to rope the Churches to the political fabric, through Communist-run front organizations. The Churches were still tightly controlled by the State Office for Church Affairs and infiltrated by secret police and by fellow travelers—religious apologists for Communism. Attempts were made to pass on to the Catholic hierarchy the task of "controlling" the Church and ensuring that it served Communist political purposes. The number of clergy declined. One movement periodically persecuted was the Bokor (Bush) Community, founded in 1948 by the Hungarian Piarist György Bulányi, with the aim of reviving local religious life and strengthening social responsibility. As for young pacifist males belonging to the Nazarene Church or to the Jehovah's Witnesses, they were still being jailed for refusing the draft in the late 1980s.

The change of system in 1989–90 brought a revival of religious activity that acted more strongly on Catholics and Jews than on Protestants. Some Catholic religious orders returned. Some small charismatic Churches sprang up. Buddhist communities and the Hare Krishna movement made their presence felt, at least in Budapest.

But conditions were far less favorable in 1990 than they had been in 1945. Two generations had grown up with little or no religious instruction. Although the Churches moved quickly to expand religious education of children, they found it hard to retain new adult members, whose churchgoing slackened off once the euphoria caused by the end of Communism was over.

CUSTOMS & TRADITIONS

HIGH DAYS AND HOLIDAYS

Hungarians love vacations. Not just their summer breaks, but the public holidays as well. The main ones are given below. Whenever possible, working days are shifted about to make a long weekend.

January 1 New Year's Day (*Újév*)

March 15 Outbreak of the 1848 Revolution and national day (*nemzeti ünnep*)

(Movable) Easter Monday and Pentecost/Whit Monday

May 1 Feast of Labor (*a munka ünnepe*) and anniversary of Hungary's entry into the E.U.

August 20 Foundation of the state, feast of St. Stephen of Hungary, and a national and state day (*nemzeti és állami ünnep*)

October 23 Anniversary of the outbreak of the 1956 Revolution and a national day (*nemzeti ünnep*)

November 1 All Saints' Day (*Mindenszentek napja*)

December 24–26 Christmas (*Karácsony*)

For instance, if a holiday falls on a Tuesday, the previous Saturday is likely to be declared a weekday and Monday treated as a Saturday. Shops will be open, but not offices or factories.

Several other days feature on the calendar of most families, including other Christian and Jewish holidays such as Ash Wednesday, Good Friday, Passover, Yom Kippur, All Souls' Day (*Halottak napja*, October 31), Hanukkah, Christmas Eve (usually known as *Szenteste*, or Holy Eve, December 24), and New Year's Eve (*Szilveszter*, December 31). Religious families may also observe Lent and Advent in various ways. Carnival *(farsang)*, between Epiphany (*Vízkereszt*, January 6) and Ash Wednesday, the first day of Lent, is the traditional period for balls and other winter festivities. Villages sometimes hold a fair *(búcsú)* on or near the dedication feast of the parish church.

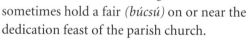

The southern town of Mohács comes alive on the last weekend before Lent, with a festival known as the *busójárás*. Folk music, craft fairs, and processions culminate on the Sunday with a parade of *busó*—mischievous men in heavy sheepskin coats and elaborate traditional wooden masks with horns. Schoolchildren observe April Fool's Day (*bolondok napja*, April 1) and are often given a chance to teach their teachers on that day. By the Danube in Budapest is one good place to be on August 20, for a morning regatta and a lavish evening fireworks display. Almost all Hungarians visit family graves before All Souls' Day (Halloween, October 31), to leave flowers and candles.

The main historical anniversaries are March 15, August 20, and October 23 (see box), but other historical events that may be marked include the liberation of Hungary from German troops in 1944 (around April 4), the signing of the 1920 Treaty of Trianon (June 4), the withdrawal of the last Soviet occupation troops in 1991 (June 30), the execution of the 1849 martyrs of Arad (October 6), and the reoccupation of Budapest by Soviet forces in 1956 (November 4). The events themselves are discussed in Chapter 1.

FAMILY OCCASIONS
Christmas (*Karácsony*)
Hungarians celebrate Christmas in much the same way as people in English-speaking countries, but the timing is different. Children traditionally clean their boots on December 5 and leave one or both of them between the leaves of a double window overnight. St. Nicholas (*Mikulás*, Santa Claus) fills them, usually with sweets, nuts, and oranges. In theory, only good children receive

presents; bad children are supposed to get a beating instead, from Krampusz, a devil figure dressed in black. The only Euro-compatible vestige of this is that a switch of gold-painted twigs is included in the Santa Claus booty. Kindergartens and schools often hold a Santa Claus celebration and may mark Christmas before they break up for the holiday.

The main festivities begin on Christmas Eve (*Szenteste)*. Shops close about midday and public transportation stops running by five o'clock. At home, the Christmas tree is decorated, and presents are placed around it. Catholic families often put a wooden Nativity group under the tree. A carol or two is sung before the presents are opened. Then there is a family supper, which traditionally includes carp or other freshwater fish, and *bejgli*, a rich cake made of pastry and filled with ground walnuts or poppy seeds.

Christmas Eve is an intimate family occasion. Any visiting among neighbors ends by about 5:00 p.m. Catholic families attend midnight mass. The time for visiting or entertaining the extended family and friends is December 25 and 26 or later in the week, as few people seem to do much work between Christmas and New Year.

New Year's Eve (*Szilveszter*)

New Year's Eve is a more sociable occasion than Christmas. Most people celebrate among friends, in someone's home, in a restaurant, or in the street. It can be a noisy occasion, with fireworks and rattles. Main streets are closed to traffic to accommodate the crowds, and public transportation in Budapest, for instance, is free. It's considered good luck to pull the tail of a piglet at New Year. Roast suckling pig is a traditional New Year's Eve dish. So are frankfurters after midnight and lentils (good luck again) next morning to banish your hangover.

Easter (*Húsvét*)

This is another big family occasion. The Easter meal on Saturday, after sunset, consists of hard-boiled eggs and ham with horseradish (grated, or grated and pickled), and a braided milk loaf called *kalács*. Most children like to stain or paint eggs for Easter Sunday breakfast. The traditional stain is onionskin, but powdered dyes in various colors are also used.

On Easter Monday, it's customary for boys and men to sprinkle girls and women they meet with a few drops of cologne. They're rewarded for this with an Easter egg (painted or chocolate) and

a peck on each cheek. Guess what! Most girls wash their hair thoroughly on Easter Monday to remove the smell of ill-chosen cologne. Earlier customs were much more exciting, with village lads splashing buckets of well water over the lasses—a folksy wet T-shirt competition, dripping with anthropological poignancy.

Other Special Days

Mother's Day *(Anyák napja)* is kept on the first Sunday in May, and Children's Day *(Gyereknap)* on the last. International Women's Day *(Nemzetközi nőnap,* March 8) is also remembered to some extent, although it's felt by some to have been a Communist invention. Father's Day and Labor Day are not known, but May Day is marked as a working-class festival, mainly by trade unionists and left-wingers, often with a *majális*—a communal outdoor picnic with stands, sideshows, and speeches—rather than the kind of mass military parade customary in the Communist period.

Wine-growing communities hold elaborate vintage celebrations in the autumn, and as many families own some vines, the grape harvest *(szüret)* and winemaking turn into other family occasions. So does pig slaughtering in

November or December, at least in the country.
Many hands are required to make all the traditional
pork products *(disznótoros)* in a single day.

Name Days
Although birthdays are celebrated, at least for
children, a person's fête or "name day" *(névnap)* is
more important to the outside world. Family,
friends, and colleagues should be greeted
personally or called on their name
day. Women often receive flowers
and men a bottle of drink or
something edible. Children
receive presents from relations
and school friends.

The first step to discovering
when friends' and colleagues' name days are
is to obtain a Hungarian calendar. However,
several common names, such as Mária, István,
and Erzsébet, have more than one name day, and
it is worth checking which of these days each
person celebrates. There's an eight-day period of
grace, within which you can still wish somebody a
happy name day.

If your name is Kylie, or Brian, for that matter,
you won't find your name in the Hungarian
calendar. Bad luck! If it bothers you, just select a
similar Hungarian name for yourself and
celebrate on the appropriate day.

FROM BIRTH TO DEATH

Hungarian babies have to be registered with
the state within eight days. Most of them receive
a single given name, but about 5 percent are
given two.

The surname comes before the given name or
names in Hungarian, but Hungarians prefer the
international order when referring to themselves
in other languages. So Kovács János becomes
János Kovács in English. Some people have
double-barreled surnames, which may be
hyphenated or not. The practice of naming a boy
after his father or godfather is common. The
father is then referred to in writing as *id.* Kovács
János (János Kovács Senior) and the son as *ifj.*
Kovács János (János Kovács Junior).

Almost half the babies born in Hungary are
baptized into the Catholic Church, sometimes
receiving an additional, baptismal name at that
time. There are normally two godparents, who are
often relatives. The ceremony may be attended by
other relatives, too, and be followed by a party in
a restaurant or at home. Most other
denominations have similar ceremonies.

Catholic children take their first communion
at a minimum age of eight and undergo
confirmation *(bérmálás)* at the age of seventeen
or eighteen, after attending religious instruction
for several years beforehand. Confirmation into

the Reformed and Evangelical (Lutheran) Churches usually comes at the age of about thirteen or fourteen. Jewish boys and girls have their bar or bat mitzvah at the age of thirteen and twelve respectively.

Hungarian weddings can be lavish, with several hundred people invited. The civil wedding takes place in a register office. About two-thirds of couples follow this with a religious ceremony of some kind. But in cities, not all those invited to the wedding ceremony are also invited to the reception. Those who are invited consult with the parents about what gift the couple would like. However, at a big traditional wedding, there will be a bride's dance: male guests asking the bride to dance place a gift of money in a hat. Go on, be generous! Make it 10,000 forints (U.S. $50). Foreign guests may need to practice the national dance, the *csárdás*, beforehand.

As yet, there is in Hungary no legal form of marriage between people of the same sex, and such marriages abroad have no legal status in Hungary.

Funerals can also be big, but usually only the immediate family or chosen friends are invited back to the house or to a restaurant. Most funerals are held at cemetery chapels, where those arriving place their flowers on or around the coffin. After the service, the coffin is taken to the grave, with the mourners following. Cremation is common and cemeteries have structures containing compartments for urns. It is customary for everyone to go over to the chief mourners and express condolences after the graveside prayers. Attendance at a funeral is an affirmation of intimacy with the bereaved family that will be noted and appreciated (see Chapter 4).

Traditionally, widows wore mourning for many months after the death of a husband, but this is observed only in villages these days.

chapter four

FRIENDS & MANNERS

Manners are closely connected with speech in Hungary, and so there are a good few Hungarian words in this chapter. Have a look at the pronunciation guide on page 158–9 if need be.

A SMILE FOR A SMILE

"The reply to a smile is a smile," as the Hungarian writer István Mácz points out. Hungary is not a closed society, just an atomized one, where personal friendship has added importance. Foreigners are welcomed into that society and appreciated. But the approach is slightly different from that of Western Europe and North America. What social relations in Hungary are mainly about is exchanging the favors, affection, support, and assistance that help people to cope with a monolithic, anonymous, inimical outside world. Quite a responsibility, in fact.

Ties of kinship and friendship are the basis of honesty and trust in Hungary, with important implications for family life, social relations, and business. Many of the friendships go back a long way. Secondary-school classmates form a network that may help them for years. As for foreign friends, they're seen as an asset. For one thing, Hungarians are interested in how things are done abroad. For another, they want to present their country and society in a favorable light, and like to do so in a subtle, indirect, self-deprecating way.

Often, foreigners in other countries have a feeling of being among people better educated than themselves. In fact, most expatriates in Hungary are highly educated and brimming with the kind of expertise that post-Communist Hungarians lack. But Hungary, like every country, has a stock of general knowledge appropriate to its society.

Foreigners hoping to integrate into Hungarian society will have to pick up some of that general knowledge and look about them. Your considered judgments about Hungary—especially if favorable!—will be music to the ears of your new Hungarian friends. So will your accounts of how things are done elsewhere.

This is not to say that nothing can be criticized in Hungarian company. There are plenty of legitimate targets: the government, the tax system, the stores, drivers, soccer managers, today's children, young people, the middle-aged, and the old. A good time will be had by all when tearing any of these to shreds. What remain sacrosanct are society itself and its fabric and customs—aspects of Hungary that can't reasonably be blamed on globalization, global warming, foreign intervention, or government stupidity. With these, tread softly, because you tread upon their dreams.

CONVERSATION AND CULTURE
Hungarians, educated or ill-educated, don't subscribe to the view increasingly found in Britain and the United States that all forms of culture are equivalent in value. They don't equate Maria Callas with Janis Joplin, as a recent BBC television series did, even if they prefer the latter. They won't put television on a par with theater, or gardening with sculpture, or value Japanese cartoon techniques such as *anime* as highly as fine art. There's still a traditional pecking order in the arts—from "high" to "middle-brow" to "low." That's not to say that Hungarians won't be fascinated to hear foreigners' arguments on the other side. They're eager customers for Hollywood films, foreign rock, British comedy, Irish music, Scandinavian design, Chinese proverbs, and even Mexican soap operas.

Conversation in Hungary covers a much wider range of subjects than it does in a British living room or pub, or American family room or bar, as Hungarians sometimes find to their cost abroad. János Kornai, a celebrated economist, spoke for many when he recalled ruefully how, as a Harvard professor, "we once had three couples to our house, including two great economists and an equally famous political scientist . . . [but] the conversation was on conventional subjects."

Which is more natural, chitchat or discourse? Leaving your work, studies, politics, artistic sensibilities, religion, and *Weltanschauung* behind before you set out to see your friends, and talking about baseball scores, car maintenance, babies, recipes, and knitting patterns instead? Or walking in and sitting down to weigh the affairs of the world or anything else that springs to mind during the conversation?

Mind you, conversation Hungarian-style is not an art learned overnight. Be careful to keep a light touch, to avoid direct contradiction, or at least phrase it in question form. Remember to show interest and respect for ideas you disagree with and if everyone's speaking English resist the temptation to use your linguistic advantage to impose your own. Hungarians, in any case, have been taught by history to be less certain than North Americans that there's a right answer to every question.

One reason, in fact, why Hungarians make witty, entertaining conversationalists is their background in the Communist system, which told you what to think and provided endless, rather facile reasons. The often circular, quibbling, specious arguments of the authorities honed people's conversational skills, turning oppression into a source of mirth. Since then, the post-Communist period and the side effects of democracy, capitalism, privatization, and globalization have provided equally inspiring subjects of discourse. Enjoy your meal!

MAKING FRIENDS

Hungarians attach great importance to friendship and file people mentally as friends, relations, or acquaintances. Friendships are long-term and have important functions in society and the economy.

There's a freemasonry among foreigners in Budapest, and "old Hungary hands" can often help you to make contact with Hungarian society as well. Budapest and several provincial towns have clubs and institutions where foreigners can meet, including national chambers of commerce and an international women's club, for instance. There are weekly newspapers that give plenty of clues as to where to find other foreigners.

Friendship for Hungarians includes effort. You put yourself out for your friends and expect them to do the same for you, even after a couple of years' gap. Hungarians are big on the symbolic value of actions, so that a small, unexpected gift or a helping hand can provide the opening to friendship. They like to rely on their friends. Early progress toward friendship may be lost by being momentarily offhand. Hungarians also need to be given opportunities to show friendship toward you. Don't shy away from imposing on them in small ways, or accepting small favors.

LANGUAGE PROBLEMS

When it comes to making friends with Hungarians, there is often a formidable language barrier with the over-thirties, who may well not have learned any English in school. A recent survey found that 35 percent of adult Hungarians were proficient in some foreign language. That may be an overestimate, or an arbitrary use of the word "proficient." The only other foreign language spoken widely is German, and a few people still speak competent Russian. There are small indigenous minorities in Hungary who between them speak about fourteen other languages.

English is entirely different from Hungarian, which makes the task of learning English rather

longer for Hungarians than for most other
Europeans. And there are two other problems.
One is shared with the British and Americans—
the absence of a language-learning culture. Few
children grow up with the example of a good
foreign-language speaker in the family, partly
because Russian, the compulsory language in
schools from the 1940s to the 1980s, was
scorned for political reasons. The other
problem is a strong dislike by Hungarians for
speaking a foreign language in front of each
other, let alone *with* each other. Foreigners in
mixed Hungarian and foreign company must
expect quite a lot of Hungarian to be spoken
around them.

That, of course, is one spur to learning the
Hungarian language. There'll be plenty of
encouragement from Hungarians, who will be
delighted with even the slightest knowledge you
may display.

"Every language is unique, the Hungarian
language is even more unique," writes Ágnes
Nemes Nagy, introducing a selection of her work
translated into English, and a few lines later, "All
poetry is untranslatable, Hungarian poetry is even
more untranslatable." But of course, the
uniqueness of a language is sensed more by its
native speakers than by those who learn it in later
life. Surely English is unique too, isn't it, and quite

untranslatable? Still, Nemes Nagy's remark is interesting as an example of the affection and pride in which Hungarians hold their language.

Be that as it may, everyday Hungarian is no more difficult or time-consuming to learn than most other foreign languages. Look on the bright side. The Roman alphabet is used. Hungarian employs few sounds that can't be pronounced reasonably well by English-speakers. Spelling is largely phonetic, and the structure of an inflected language like Hungarian is easy to pin down because its rules can neatly be captured in tables and other visual aids.

BEHAVIOR

Good manners begin with a greeting. Stand up! Only the old and frail stay seated for greetings. The practice in Hungary is for a man to make the first greeting to a woman, a younger person to an older, a subordinate to a superior, a salesperson to a customer, and someone entering or approaching to those already present. It's bad manners not to greet people, and worse not to return a greeting.

Having begun the chapter with smiles, it should be said at this point that Hungarians don't usually smile at strangers, because it seems too familiar. Americans in particular are startled by the somber expressions they may meet with in

Hungarian stores and restaurants, misinterpreting them as rudeness or indifference. But go into a store or restaurant a second time, and there's likely to be a nod or even a smile to accompany the greeting.

People meeting for the first time give a formal handshake and exchange names. They may also mutter "*Örvendek*" ("Delighted"). There's no need for a third party to effect an introduction. A visiting card is worth offering if you have one, as it's hard for both sides to catch foreign names the first time around.

It's customary to shake hands with everyone, known or unknown, if you're entering a meeting or group. Men or women kiss women on each cheek if they know them socially, and even at work, but only silver-haired roués kiss a woman's hand these days. Today there's no need for men to click their heels as they bow, impressive though this looks in pre-war Hungarian movies. Male relatives may kiss each other, but this won't be expected of foreigners. Even teenagers among themselves observe some of these customs. Adults should include older children in greetings rituals, unless they're obviously hanging back. Foreign children should be encouraged to join in, too.

A plain greeting (no handshake) is also given to strangers as you enter or leave an elevator or a railway compartment, but not a bus or a streetcar. If you have to share a table in a restaurant or cafeteria, the correct greetings are "*Jó étvágyat!*" "(*Bon appetit!*)" to those already eating when you arrive, "*További jó étvágyat!*" ("Further *bon appetit!*") to those still at it when you stand up to go, and "*Egészségére!*" ("To your health!") to people finishing their meal.

LOST FOR WORDS

The problem for Hungarians meeting foreigners is that many of the nuances of behavior vanish if Hungarian is not being spoken. This leaves them uncomfortable about how to behave. The degrees of familiarity in Hungarian range from using the second person (to relations, friends, children, or animals) to the third person with the name of the person addressed, or a pronoun (there are two, one more formal than the other).

Hungarians who speak good English may know that they should address strangers as Mr. or Mrs., but it goes against the grain with them to do so, because the equivalent forms in Hungarian are not particularly polite.

Nine times out of ten, Hungarians who are acquainted call each other by their given names, expressing familiarity or politeness simply by their use of the second or third person. When the name is not known, or if extra politeness of address is required, a Hungarian might say, "*mérnök úr*" ("Mr. Engineer"), "*szomszéd úr*" ("Mr. Neighbor"), *tanárnő* ("Ms. Teacher"), or *igazgató asszony* ("Mrs. Manager"). None of these forms translates well into English, which can leave Hungarians lost for words. Foreigners should quickly put people out of their misery by suggesting their given name, as in, "Please call me Jack," and asking, "What can I call you?"

The problem is compounded with married women. In many cases, they take their husband's full name when they marry. For example, on marrying János Kovács (Kovács János in Hungarian), Gabriella Takács becomes Kovács Jánosné, and "Gabriella" doesn't even feature in her ID! Well, that has to be translated as Mrs. János Kovács. The alternatives open to brides these days are Gabriella Kovács (Kovács Gabriella) or not changing her name at all (quite common).

ADDRESSING PEOPLE
Hungarian greetings and forms of address are worth learning. Taking the polite forms first, *csókolom* (an abbreviation of "I kiss your hand") is used when meeting and saying good-bye, by

men to women, and by children to grown-ups. Otherwise the usual greetings between strangers or those on formal terms would be *jó reggelt kívánok* ("Good morning") early in the morning, *jó napot kívánok* ("Good day") until early evening, *jó estét kívánok* ("Good evening") thereafter, and *jó éjszakát* ("Good night") if someone's off to bed. Another fairly formal greeting between acquaintants is *üdvözlöm* ("I greet you"). The commonest farewell is *viszontlátásra* ("Till we see each other again").

The familiar form of address—known as *tegezés*, from *te,* the Hungarian second person singular pronoun—is indicated by its use in a verb, and is used to and among children and young adults, between women of similar age, relations, and familiar friends, in the last case, after they have specifically agreed to do so. Normally a suggestion of being on familiar terms would come from a woman to a man, or an older person to a younger. Some less well-educated Hungarians appear to think that foreigners are children because they can't speak Hungarian properly, and accordingly go for *tegezés*. This should usually be gracefully accepted! However, *tegezés* is the form for insults as well. Lip-readers testify that car drivers always use the familiar forms when suggesting how pedestrians or other drivers should behave.

It's impolite to return the wrong greeting—
either to adopt familiarity unasked or to spurn
familiarity proffered by others, unless you can
somehow imply that you're not worthy of the
honor. Foreigners who accidentally use a familiar
form in addressing someone may find that the
Hungarian instantly accepts it, and no harm done,
but it's not an elegant mistake!

Another point: being on familiar terms
with one of a married couple doesn't
automatically mean you're on familiar terms
with the other, let alone their grown-up
children. *Tegezés* between adults is symmetrical,
so that if older people use it to people much
younger than themselves, aside from very
young children, they may put the younger
person in a spot. The last thing the young want
is to seem familiar to Daddy's business
partner, for instance. They may even get the
unfortunate impression that they're being
treated like a child.

What forms of address are used at work
will depend on the boss. It would be odd if
those of the same sex who were involved in a
common project—say on an informal
committee—didn't go for *tegezés*. The same
would apply to people helping each other to
build a house, kill a pig, make a patchwork
quilt, or mend a motorcycle.

NODS AND BOWS

Being on familiar terms may imply frankness, friendship, or identity of aims, but it doesn't necessarily imply equality, so if you address your boss in the familiar form, as requested, a little extra politeness may be in order. A nod or a slight bow, or introducing what you have to say with a formula such as, "excuse me for disturbing you," will make the boss think what a well-mannered person this new young foreigner is, and what a pleasure it is to have him or her in the firm.

One way to sidestep these problems, you might think, is to stick to English, but it doesn't really resolve them, because it leaves your relationships awkwardly undefined in terms of degree of politeness, at least for Hungarians. So greeting people in Hungarian is a good habit to cultivate. It also gives you useful information about how they feel about their relationship with you. Stammering out a "*Jó napot kívánok*" (formal), and getting a smile and an emphatic "*Szervusz*" (familiar) in reply, means that you can be a bit more friendly than you thought.

Actually, the smart way to say good-bye in Hungarian is to use a phrase appropriate to the situation. Just a few of the many: *jó pihenést* ("Have a good rest," said to people leaving work), *jó munkát* ("Good work"), *jó mulatást* ("Have fun"), *jó kirándulást* ("Good trip").

Children may address men as *X bácsi* and women as *Xnéni*. Adults do the same to people twenty or more years older than themselves, even if they are on familiar second-person terms. This should be avoided with ladies of a certain age who have taken great care with their appearance, or still play tennis in a geriatric sort of way. Men can have the extra-polite formula *X bátyám* up their sleeve for immensely eminent men with whom they're on familiar terms—your wife's godfather, or an elderly high-court judge, say.

The point of all this is the usefulness of taking some Hungarian lessons if you're going to be living in Hungary for a while. Even if you speak English with your friends and colleagues, a good Hungarian teacher is an invaluable source of information on how to behave politely. A teacher, by the way, is addressed as *tanár úr* if male and *tanárnő* if female, with plenty of earnest nods and not too many have-a-good-day smiles, unless known very well. Actors, artists, musicians, opera singers, ballet dancers, contortionists, and trapeze artists are addressed as *művész úr* or *művésznő*.

Hello and Good-bye

Most of the many, many familiar words for hello in Hungarian also mean good-bye. The commonest hail or farewell between adults on familiar terms is *szervusz,* derived from the Latin *servus*, servant. Alternatives are *szia, szevasz,* and *szerbusz.* In fact *szia* and, increasingly, *helló*, are probably the commonest familiar greetings heard today.

That's only the tip of the iceberg. Young or earnestly cool people use endless, sometimes short-lived alternatives—*szeva, szió, szióka, sziamia,* and *sziómió* come from *szervusz. Helló* (even on departure), *hellóka, helóbeló, hahó, holi,* and *holihó* form another group, but it's worth noting that *halló* means something different: it's used for calling someone across a field or a telephone line.

Csáo, csá, csácsumi, csákány, cső, csocsesz, csocsi, csovi, csőváz, and *csumi* are among the commoner *ciao* derivatives. *Puszi, pusszancs,* and similar words simply mean a peck on the cheek. A truncated *pá* ("bye") is used by elderly ladies as a farewell.

Hungarian is flexible—just follow suit!

chapter five

HUNGARIANS AT HOME

HOUSE AND HOME

Many visitors to Hungary are struck by the poor condition of residential buildings. The shabby apartment blocks in cities and tumbledown houses in villages make a sharp contrast with neighboring Austria, for example. But however scruffy the block may look, step into a Budapest apartment and you're likely to enter a spotless, well-decorated, and comfortable home. Hungarian housewives spend more time on their homes than their counterparts in any other nation in Europe.

The poor maintenance of buildings applies especially to the big apartment blocks in Budapest and other cities, which were sold by the state to their tenants at rock-bottom prices some fifteen years ago. Owners have since found it difficult to reach agreement among themselves on maintenance costs or to chase down those who neglect to pay. Maintenance charges remain low, as a glance at halls, stairways, and elevators shows. This applies equally to fine late-nineteenth-century houses and to shoddy 1960s and '70s tower blocks.

Most Hungarians live in what people in English-speaking countries would class as cramped conditions: an average of only 323 sq. ft (30 sq. m) per person. A room may often serve two or more purposes—such as a living room and study by day, and a bedroom by night. Almost 40 percent of the dwellings in Hungary are apartments.

Wholesale privatization of housing in the 1990s has left about 95 percent of homes owned privately (almost all by their occupants) and 5 percent publicly owned. This is about the same proportion as in Germany (6 percent), but much lower than the 20 percent proportion of "social rented housing" in the U.K. Although tenants were able to buy their homes at rock-bottom prices, they were not prepared for the true cost of running them. Now about 20 percent of the new condominiums are in financial straits.

The number of new homes built each year has doubled since 1990 to over 60,000, but only about 30 percent of new homes are built and sold by commercial contractors. Most are put up by the families who will live in them, hiring skilled labor as they need it and doing much of the drudgery themselves.

Much of central Budapest consists of traditional, six-story, late-nineteenth-century apartment blocks. The typical block is built around one or more courtyards, with a grand staircase on the street side and access to the apartments along iron gangways running around on each floor. Unlike the similar blocks in most European countries, they were built for a broad social mix of tenants. The ground floor on the street side was given over to shops or workshops. The concierge *(házmester)* and his assistant *(vice)* lived modestly in dank, single-room dwellings at the back of the ground floor. The cheapest apartments were on the uppermost floors at the back, and the largest and most expensive, with the highest ceilings, were on the lower levels, on the street side of the house. A grand apartment consisted of up to six interconnecting rooms, a kitchen, a bathroom, and servants' quarters. Most of these large apartments were divided up after the Second World War, but the mansions survive, and apartments of this kind can still be found for rent or sale.

One excellent example of a mansion flat now contains the Budapest Postal Museum. The house (VI. Andrássy út 3.) is a fine turn-of-the-century building, complete with lavishly molded and decorated ceilings, warm paneling, and frescoes in the stairwell by Károly Lotz, whose work can also be seen in the Opera and Parliament.

RENTING AND BUYING

Hungarians don't like to move. Three-generation households are common, and many people still live in the far from convenient homes in which they were born. One reason for this reluctance is the imperfection of the housing market. Hungarians who do offer their home for sale tend to have vague, optimistic ideas of how much it's worth and prove hard to deal with.

Walk into a U.K. or U.S. real estate agent's office and you'll be told fairly accurately what your property is worth, according to its location and condition. But there's a touch of magic here. The pricing system works mainly because sellers believe in it and do as they're told.

Real estate agents in Hungary have none of that prestige and show little of the professionalism of their Western counterparts. Many vendors try to do without a real estate agent, or collude with the purchaser to avoid paying the agent's fees.

This is not easy ground to negotiate, but increasing numbers of foreigners have been buying property in Hungary. A generally rising market in the last couple of decades has masked many of their mistakes. There are still bargains to be had in the Hungarian housing market, and the administrative obstacles are not great, for E.U. citizens at least. But it's unwise even to start searching without a structural engineer *(statikus)* and a lawyer *(ügyvéd)* behind you. Hungarian building-trade workers are immensely charming and inventive, but there are good reasons why most foreign buyers choose a newly completed or renovated property.

The small market for rented accommodation is better organized, but uncertainties remain. Prospective tenants should compare rents carefully before signing a contract and go for a new or newly renovated property where possible. The state of the Hungarian housing stock means that in most cases, landlords and tenants have quite close, ongoing relationships during the tenancy. The probable maintenance and other problems mean that a good landlord–tenant relationship can make a big difference.

It's worth sizing up the landlord or landlady personally and making sure it's possible for the two sides to communicate easily before signing a contract. Landlords generally look for something like six months' or a year's rent upfront, as an advance and/or a deposit, so that remedying a bad choice can turn out to be expensive later.

THE FAMILY

In most Hungarian families both the husband and the wife work outside the home. On average, men work longer hours than women, often taking a second job on the side, but women do most of the work around the house.

Quite a high proportion of Hungarian families involve grandparents in bringing up children. Three-generation households are common, as we have seen, but many other parents send their children to country grandparents in the summer.

Children are watched and pampered in a way that their peers in Western Europe or North America would find odd. Where parents are able to do so, they follow their children's school studies very closely, often helping them with homework.

Young teenagers in middle-class families attend organized activities on weekday afternoons—sports, extra lessons, music, and so on. This leaves them comparatively little time to develop the kind of youth subcultures found in Western Europe and North America. Their weekends are dominated by family chores, visits, and activities. Saturday or babysitting jobs are unknown.

EDUCATION

Education has burgeoned in the last decade, as the number of children has declined. Most parents like their own children to have as much education as possible—but they don't always feel the same way about everybody else's children. In other words, there is widespread doubt in society about the extra years that children are spending at school and college.

Children must either have completed eight years of schooling or have reached their sixteenth birthday before leaving school. Formal school starts at the age of six, but most have attended kindergarten for up to three years by that age.

There are three tiers of education. Elementary schools normally provide eight grades of primary education. Then come four years of secondary education.

Teaching is more formal than in schools in English-speaking countries. The *érettségi*, or graduation (school-leaving) certificate, is normally taken in four to seven subjects, including Hungarian, math, history, and a foreign language. Grades resulting from these exams, and from the last two years' schoolwork, are the basis for deciding who will be admitted to study what in higher education.

Nowadays, 90 percent of sixteen-year-olds are still in full-time education. Of these, 23 percent go on to follow vocational courses that offer only a skill, not an *érettségi*; 43 percent follow vocational courses that include an *érettségi*; and 34 percent are at gymnasia, or academically oriented secondary schools.

Some gymnasia offer a year's intensive language learning before the ninth grade and then use two languages of instruction for the four-year secondary course. This means that most subjects, apart from Hungarian and history, are taught in the foreign language. There are fee-paying American, German, French, Japanese, and other international schools in Budapest.

There are almost three hundred schools run by religious organizations. These teach about 4 percent of the children in school. (Under the Communists, there were only eight Church-run schools in the whole country.) These religious schools receive much the same funds from the state budget as the state schools do, mainly in the form of "capitation" grants per child enrolled.

There are a handful of private primary and secondary schools. Boarding schools in the British or American sense are hardly known, but students living far from their schools are given subsidized hostel (*kollégium*) accommodation nearby.

About 40 percent of twenty-year-olds are still in full-time higher education, taking three-year college courses or university courses lasting four to six years.

Sweet Sorrow

Students in their last year of high school have a busy time. As if the all-important final exams weren't enough, there are other matters to attend to.

First comes the Ribbon Inauguration Ball (*szalagavató bál*), usually in the autumn, to which families are invited. Each graduate receives a ribbon with the years of attendance on it, and it's worn proudly in the lapel for the rest of the school year. Each final-year class has spent months preparing a display dance, often rather daring and modern. Then a quick change, and the teenagers are transformed into full ballroom regalia, to dance a perfect Viennese waltz straight out of operetta. Not a dry eye in the house. A tableau is made with photographs of the classes and their teachers. This is usually displayed in a local shop.

Next comes the Parade (*ballagás*) in May. Classrooms and corridors are decorated with flowers. The graduates form a file, each with a hand on the shoulder in front, and shuffle through the whole school, laden with the flowers thrust upon them, singing "Gaudeamus igitur," and other traditional songs. The eleventh-graders have prepared for each graduate a little party bag containing a forint coin to symbolize wealth, some salt to work up a thirst for knowledge, and a savory scone for their journey into the wide world. More tears are shed. Between the end of the parade and the end of the exams, graduates may visit the teachers at home, serenading them from the street, then enjoying an evening of talking, eating, drinking, and reminiscing. Finally comes a restaurant banquet, and arrangements are made for everyone to meet up in one, five, ten, twenty, and fifty years' time.

LOVE AND SEXUALITY

Love and sexuality are eagerly and frankly discussed in Hungary, but on the whole, the attitudes are more conservative than in Western Europe. This applies especially to the young and those who look after them.

The age of consent for voluntary sexual activity between persons of different sexes is fourteen, but this is misleading. Girls are normally seen as off-limits to their peers and to adults until they finish school at about eighteen. Families may try to stop relationships developing between teenagers, in case they "get out of hand" or interfere with schoolwork. Hungarians may marry at eighteen, or at sixteen with permission from a parent or guardian. The age of consent for voluntary homosexual activity is also eighteen, and this is the lower legal age limit for "sex workers."

So Hungarians tend to be less adventurous and experienced in love than those in Western Europe or North America. Some 7 percent of babies are born to mothers under the age of twenty, but almost all of these young mothers have had only eight or fewer years of formal education. The schoolbag acts as a powerful taboo.

Condoms can be bought freely at a pharmacy (*gyógyszertár*) or supermarket. Contraceptive and morning-after pills are available by prescription. The number of induced abortions has halved since the mid-1970s, but so have births, so that over 35 percent of pregnancies are still being artificially terminated.

Prostitutes soliciting outdoors are harassed by the police, and brothels as such are illegal. Most of the sex trade is therefore underground, which puts foreign customers especially at some risk of theft or overcharging. But the trade thrives, nonetheless. Hotel porters, taxi drivers, coy flyposting, small ads in the press, and soliciting in bars are the main marketing tools.

Children these days don't appear naked in public after they start school at the age of six, but most parents are relaxed about nudity until signs of puberty appear. Most Hungarians find adult nudity distasteful, although there are several nudist bathing places, including Omszki-tó and Délegyháza on the borders of Budapest.

Teenagers themselves seem to place emphasis on establishing a relationship, where they can, rather than on group activity with a sexual content. Although almost all schools are mixed, boys and girls don't reintegrate fully until their mid-teens. They have fewer opportunities than English-speaking teenagers for casual sex, which is associated with low social status.

Awareness of the risks of pedophilia and other sexual violence has increased substantially in the last twenty years. Traveling on public transportation and walking home, often before the parents are back, Hungarian children may appear to be at greater risk than their English-speaking peers, who are so often ferried around in cars. But the statistics match those of Western Europe: risks for children from violence and abuse are much higher within the family than outside it.

Hungarians are likely to intervene if they see children in trouble, misbehaving, or being ill-treated. On the whole, kids by themselves, or in pairs at least, appear to behave better in public than some of their counterparts in the U.K. or France, for instance. But adult protectiveness ceases rather suddenly at puberty. Irate adult passengers quarrel with teenagers on the bus for scarcely perceptible misdemeanors.

MARRIAGE

Marriage in Hungary is often postponed or avoided altogether. The average age for marriage has risen by about four years since 1990, to twenty-eight for men and twenty-six for women. (There have been similar rises, to thirty for men and twenty-eight for women, in the U.K.) Over 40 percent of marriages end in divorce. (This compares with 55 percent in the U.S.A. and the U.K.)

There is no stigma attached to being born out of wedlock, and little of the social disapproval of cohabitation found in some sections of U.K. and U.S. society. Almost half the twenty- to twenty-four-year-olds in partnership relations with someone of the opposite sex are unmarried. Even among thirty- to thirty-four-year-olds the proportion is almost 15 percent.

The number of children born every year has fallen by almost 30 percent since 1990. Hungary's population has declined from a peak of 10.7 million in the early 1980s to lower than 10.1 million today. The number of children falls as the standard of living rises in most developed societies, but this happened earlier and to a greater than average extent in Hungary. There is strong public awareness of the "demographic problem," especially the future burden of looking after the aged. Almost everyone supports the idea of families having two or three children, but fewer, when it comes down to it, actually do so themselves, mainly because they feel their home would be cramped and they are afraid of the financial sacrifices involved. Large families are almost entirely confined to the urban rich and the rural "underclass."

For the population to reproduce itself, every 100 women would need to give birth to 210 children. The present birthrate translates into a mere 130 children. The shortfall is partly offset by the fact that people are living longer. Life expectancy at birth has risen to sixty-eight for men and seventy-seven for women (against seventy-five and eighty-one in the U.K. and U.S., seventy-seven and eighty-four in Canada, and seventy-eight and eighty-three in Australia). The small surplus of immigration over emigration makes no appreciable difference.

So Hungarians are living longer, but marrying less readily and having fewer children, so that the population is aging. According to one tongue-in-cheek projection, the last Hungarian will die of old age in about four thousand years' time.

PETS

Most families in Hungary seem to keep a dog and be quite fond of it, though, paradoxically, the dogs are not looked after very well. Many dogs are kept outside, sometimes chained. While today the dog's life is improving, visitors should remember that stress can give dogs short tempers.

TIME OUT

People in Hungary earn much less than they do in the English-speaking countries—but they don't let it worry them. Many compensate by working overtime or taking a second job, which cuts deeply into their leisure time. That being said, the basic working week in most jobs is forty to forty-eight hours long, and employees have a good vacation entitlement of three to five weeks.

BACK TO THE LAND

They call it a *dacha* in Russia and a *gîte* in France. Hungarians call it a *nyaraló*. It may simply be a

patch of garden with a toolshed, but there is often a cottage where its owners can sleep. In fact, some of these "cottages" are positively luxurious—proper houses with swimming pools, wine cellars, vineyards, orchards, and superb views.

Many Hungarians are first- or second-generation city dwellers. A *nyaraló* allows them to get back to their roots, to cultivate a little land, to sit in the sun, to make strawberry jam or pick apples, to go swimming or fishing, or to natter over the fence to neighbors. The owners are usually part of an extended family, in which the older members do much of the gardening and maintenance, and perhaps move to the *nyaraló* for the whole summer, often joined by children and grandchildren.

The most popular locations are around Balaton, Lake Velence, or the Danube Bend, but *nyaraló* settlements can be seen on hillsides all over the country. That is where millions of Hungarian city dwellers most like to be, and where they do their summer entertaining.

SPORTS AND PASTIMES

Most Hungarians enjoy watching sports on television, but relatively few of them take part after the age of twenty-five. By far the most popular spectator sport is soccer *(foci)*. The legendary Golden Team *(aranycsapat)* walked off with the 1952 Olympic trophy and trounced England 6–3 at Wembley, for the first time ever, in 1953, before beating them 7–1 at home the next year and reaching the World Championship finals. To put it another way, the

Golden Team scored 220 goals in fifty-one matches between June 1950 and November 1955—but "how are the mighty fallen." The national team has had no appreciable international success since 1986, when it managed to qualify for the World Championships in Mexico. Most Hungarian club soccer matches today attract pitiful crowds of a couple of hundred, although television ratings are still high, with one or two matches shown in full every weekend during the season (August to November and March to June). Meanwhile, several hundred Hungarians (sometimes known as the Foreign Legion) play professional football abroad.

However, there are several sports in which Hungary often does well in world championships and at the Olympics: canoeing, handball, water polo, swimming, pentathlon, fencing, and shooting, for instance.

The focuses of sports in Hungary are the sports clubs all over the country, which may cover both amateur and professional players and run teams in a wide range of sports. Many clubs are centered on Hungarian League soccer teams. These clubs have plenty of facilities for sports at an amateur level. So do local clubs, often attached to a school gym, and you don't need to

be connected with the school to take part. All
these facilities are cheap by European or North
American standards.

There are six eighteen-hole golf courses in the
Budapest area with open member-
ship, although green fees are
set at international levels.
Riding and tennis are readily
available, popular, and quite
reasonably priced. One place of
pilgrimage for horse riders is
Szilvásvárad, a small town 19 miles (30 km) from
Eger, and famous for its stud of Lipizzaner horses.

There is good windsurfing, kitesurfing,
and sailing on Lake Balaton, and
waterskiing on Lake Tisza. Attractive
places for canoeing include the
Szigetköz stretch of the Danube and
around the wine region of Tokaj,
on the River Tisza. From October to
February you can skate on the lake in the
Városliget, a park in the middle of Budapest.
There are smaller rinks at several shopping
centers. Ten-pin bowling is popular, and is also
played competitively.

There are 250 chess clubs affiliated with the
Hungarian Chess Federation *(Magyar Sakkszövetség)*.
There are plenty of people to play a game of chess
with you in the summer in Budapest parks.

SAVING AND SPENDING

Shops and banks have improved beyond all recognition in the last fifteen years, but they still leave something to be desired. So shopping, unlike chess, hardly counts as a sport yet in Hungary.

Banking services are still relatively crude and expensive, often attracting mysterious charges and offering a minimal or negative real rate of interest on deposits. Advice on investment in Hungary is best sought from specialist brokers. Government securities are a better bargain, most of the time, than most of the schemes banks offer.

After initial experiences, many foreigners draw logical conclusions and transfer only the most necessary aspects of their banking to Hungary, leaving the rest to be handled from home. The biggest bank for personal accounts is the OTP, but there are several others. Expect to wait in line to see a teller. The lowest charges are usually found at a savings cooperative (*takarékszövetkezet*), but many offer only limited services. Some banking services are offered in post offices.

Shopping malls and hypermarkets have taken over from traditional shopping areas in Hungary more completely than they have in most other European countries. Malls certainly have convenience and variety on their side, but the shops in them tend to be more expensive than the solo hypermarkets on the edge of towns.

The most enjoyable places to shop are the market halls of Budapest and some other cities. The units vary from full-scale shops to one little peasant woman selling a handful of vegetables or a few jars of honey. At the Central Market Hall (*Nagycsarnok*) of Pest there are ten or twelve rival traders selling live freshwater fish, and even an Asian deli in the basement. The snack stands on the iron galleries above are among the best fast-food bargains in the city. Go native and order wine and soda *(fröccs)* to wash them down.

Also enjoyable are the craft markets held from time to time in the Buda Castle District and elsewhere, especially in the summer. There's a big Christmas one in Vörösmarty tér, in the center of Pest—avoid the mulled wine if you're carrying pottery you've just bought!

INTO THE COUNTRYSIDE

There are marked trails for hikers in many country areas, especially woodland. These marks, painted on trees and walls, are shown on special hiking maps, but often by the initial of the color in Hungarian (K=blue, S=yellow, P=red, Z=green). The longest and most celebrated trail is

the Blue Tour (*Kék túra*), which stretches right
across the country.

Among the handiest and most popular areas for
a walk on the wild side are the Buda Hills,
overlooking Budapest. For instance, there's a good
trail (yellow signs) leading up from the terminus of
the 56 tram at Hüvösvölgy through the woods,
taking in three hilltop lookout towers: Kis-Hárs-
hegy (a rickety wooden double helix) and Nagy-
Hárs-hegy (sturdier), and after crossing a main
road at Szépjuhászné and taking the red trail, the
stone tower on the peak of János-hegy. You can
then return on the chairlift *(libegő)* to Zugliget
and the 158 bus back to town, having enjoyed at
least four superb views of the city and its
surroundings. A hiking map of the Buda Hills
(A Budai-hegység turistatérképe) and similar
maps for other scenic areas are widely
available.

Urban cycling is still in its infancy. Although
Budapest has 90 miles (140 km) of cycle paths,
they are lightly used and often obstructed by
pedestrians and parked cars. The rest of the
country is crisscrossed by designated
cycle paths or recommended
country lanes, shown on
several national road atlases.
One good trip is an Austro-
Hungarian ride around Lake

Fertő—reasonably flat, very scenic, and a total of about 80–90 miles (130–40 km), with plenty of beaches and facilities by the wayside. Renting a bike usually costs about 2,000 forints (U.S. $10) a day.

There are plenty of riding stables throughout Hungary, offering horses for experienced riders and lessons for novices. Prices are cheaper than in Western Europe. For instance, it's possible to keep your own horse at a riding stable for as little as 50,000 forints ($240) a month.

Hungary is also an ideal place for bird-watching. It has a wide range of habitats and lies at a crossroads of busy migration routes. Some 350 species are observed regularly. The best guide is Gerard Gorman's *Birds of Hungary*, which can be picked up from Internet booksellers.

There are well-stocked lakes, rivers, and reservoirs for freshwater fishing throughout Hungary, and catches are famous for their variety and flavor. Fishing seasons vary for species and locations. Licenses are bought locally and reasonably priced. The sport is very popular with Hungarians.

Hunting (which means shooting, not chasing by huntsmen and hounds, which is not practiced) has deep roots in Hungary. The game includes roe and red deer, wild boar, moufflon (wild sheep),

and various birds and waterfowl. Permanent
residents may take the hunting exam, buy
third-party insurance, and join
the Hungarian National Hunting
Chamber. Visitors must present a
home hunting license to the
Chamber. Unfortunately, it is not
legal at present to rent guns;
prospective hunters must have their own.

Rock climbers, beginners or experienced, will
find plenty of interesting cliff faces and artificial
climbing walls—there's even one in the
Amusement Park (*Vidámpark*) in Budapest, and
some schools have them.

Off the Beaten Track
Rural Hungary is sparsely populated and uniquely
attractive. One type of house that visitors to
Hungary often find enticing is the traditional
peasant cottage. Each district has its own variant,
but in most parts it consists of two or three rooms
and a kitchen arranged side by side, at right angles
to the road, on a relatively long, narrow plot of
land. Farm buildings, orchard, and a narrow strip
of farmland continue beyond. An open fire with a
smoke hole in the roof above the kitchen gave way
to a stove and a proper chimney in the early
twentieth century. Walls are often made of mud
bricks on a masonry foundation, and roofs may

be of thatch, or tiles, or occasionally shingles.

There is a complete village of such cottages at Hollókő in Nógrád County, all built in traditional style after a fire in 1909, in the folk style of the district. They are grouped around a tiny church in the shadow of a ruined medieval castle. Several of them are available to rent. Typical cottages and country buildings have been transported from various parts of the country and rebuilt as a national open-air museum (*skanzen*) outside Szentendre, twenty miles north of Budapest. There are similar local collections in Szombathely and elsewhere, but almost all Hungarian villages still have some traditional cottages.

Doing up a country cottage is popular among wealthier Hungarians and foreign buyers. There are long traditions of Hungarians owning a small garden or a second home if they can afford it. Acquiring such a piece of rural Hungary of your own can be a rewarding experience.

BALATON

Lake Balaton has an area of 232 square miles (600 sq. km), a length of 48 miles (77 km), a breadth of 1–9 miles (1.5–14 km), a depth of less than 13 feet (4 m) in most places and nowhere more than 38 feet (11.5 m), and a shoreline of around 125 miles (200 km)—but saying all this is to miss the point. Balaton ("Balcsi" to its friends) is more than a lake, it's a state of mind. Although more people go to the Adriatic coast than to Balaton nowadays, it's still synonymous to Hungarians with a traditional summer vacation on the beach.

The season is only eight to ten weeks long, prices are fairly high (for Hungary), the beaches are sometimes crowded, and many of the forty or so resorts are nondescript in appearance, but choose carefully (Balatonfüred, Balatonföldvár, Tihany, or the hilly shore onwards to Keszthely), and Balaton will work its magic. The nearest resorts are less than sixty miles from Budapest.

The water is silky, a slightly milky gray, and as clean as the Adriatic. It heats up to 77–80°F (25–27°C) or more on a summer's day. And in winter—another good time for a visit—it freezes quickly for skating or gadding about on the local type of hand-pulled sleigh—a *fakutya* or "wooden dog," really a kitchen chair on runners propelled with short ski sticks, often with help from a skater.

Vacationing at Balaton began in a modest way in the early nineteenth century, around such places as Balatonfüred, which has medicinal springs said to be good for heart disease. The Helikon arts festival at Keszthely took place for the first time in 1817. Bathing in the lake itself became popular with the wealthy in the 1830s. Balaton vacations became affordable for all in the Communist period, if not available to all at the trade union hostels that mushroomed in the 1960s. Vouchers were distributed to "workers," largely according to an elaborate system of sociopolitical points. Many of these hostels still survive, offering simple accommodation with full board at reasonable cost, usually to members of a company, institution, association, or school.

A Present Idea

The atmosphere of the early years of Balaton tourism is charmingly captured on a coffee service first produced at Hungary's Herend Porcelain Manufactory in about 1860. Each piece shows a different Balaton scene. Lucky Emperor-King Francis Joseph and his consort, Elizabeth, were given a service for their coronation in 1867.

You too can buy one. Hand-shaped and exquisitely hand-painted, it's in Herend's special-products catalog, at a little over U.S. $20,000.

FOOD AND DRINK
Country Cooking

This section is about what Hungarians actually eat, especially in the country and on the weekend, when there is time to cook. It's not about what they might serve to a rich uncle from America, or what a sophisticated restaurant would provide for foreign patrons. But it gives some indication of the food and drink that may be found on the menu of an unpretentious, traditional restaurant.

Families are said to spend, on average, around a third of their disposable income on food and drink. One puzzling statistic shows that older people spend more than younger, but the explanation may be that Hungarians often visit the old folks at home for traditional meals on weekends. If you're ever invited to join them, don't miss the opportunity.

When possible, Hungarians like to eat their main meal in the middle of the day and have cold food in the evening. A typical Hungarian lunch consists of soup and a main course. The sweet course is often left out, but several popular main courses and even some soups are sweet.

The meats of choice are fresh or smoked pork, and chicken. Beef is regularly eaten boiled or stewed, but less often grilled, as top-quality beef is expensive. Goose, duck, and lamb are occasionally eaten. So are venison, wild boar, and other game.

Hungarians are not great fish eaters. Apart from frozen sea fish, the popular choices are carp, salmon, trout, and *fogas*, a kind of pike-perch, a Lake Balaton delicacy—but many Hungarians prefer to let a restaurant cope with them.

Fishermen's soup *(halászlé)* is an exception. It's a spicy brew, dark red with paprika, and should include two or more types of fish, including roe. It's often cooked outside in a cauldron, and is also eaten by many families at Christmastime. The classic soup otherwise is a consommé of chicken, beef, or pork *(húsleves)*, with vermicelli and plenty of vegetables—carrot, parsley root, celeriac, and onion are the staples. Soup, noodles, and vegetables are placed on the table separately, and diners compile their own bowlful.

On the whole, the Hungarian idea of a square meal is something that's been cooked for a long time in a good, thick, spicy sauce, with plenty of potato, rice, gnocchi, dumplings, or pasta, and something pickled. Outsize gherkins are popular, pickled in the conventional way in winter, but in summer, often just left out in the sun in a jar with some fennel and a piece of bread in the liquor, to make "leavened" cucumbers *(kovászos uborka)*.

Salads take over from pickles in summer and early autumn. These are normally served individually—

tomato *or* bell pepper *or* lettuce *or* cucumber—as a side dish in a mild liquor of vinegar, water, sugar, and salt. Cucumbers are sometimes given a thicker, pink dressing by adding spice paprika, pepper, and sour cream. The yellow bell peppers can be stronger than they look. Another specialty is a large, flat,

sweet, dark-red bell pepper, *paradicsom-paprika* (tomato pepper), with especially thick flesh. The round or pointed chili-like peppers are used in cooking, or ground fresh and added to goulash or fishermen's soup. They can be bought on a string like garlic and hung up in the kitchen.

Garlic, paprika, and marjoram are the commonest flavorings used. The stock cubes of Western Europe are joined in Hungary by goulash cubes and fishermen's-soup cubes.

Sausages of all kinds are eaten cooked or cured. The most famous abroad are Hungarian salami and hard sausages such as *csabai* and *gyulai*. Hungarians themselves probably eat more boiled sausage than any other. *Debreceni*, a thick, fairly spicy, garlicky sausage, is often sold hot at the butcher's, with mild mustard and fresh bread.

Killing a pig is an all-day family occasion, in which the squeamish should not become

involved. The fruits of the labor are a
bewildering variety of pork products
that can be hung up in the cellar to last
a country family through the winter,
including bacon, chaps, brawn, blood
and liver sausage for roasting, harder sausage for
storing, pork for roasting, and fat for cooking.
The traditional main course at the pig-killing feast
consists of blood sausage, liver sausage, garlic
sausage, and roast pork, accompanied by boiled
potatoes with onions, and stewed cabbage.

Bread, Cheese, and Bacon
Bread is a big and rewarding subject in Hungary.
It's eaten at breakfast, lunch, and supper.
Hungarians don't share the Anglo-Saxon view that
brown bread is morally and nutritionally superior
to white. Bread should be white and firm, they say,
and in Hungary at least, they're probably right. The
brown bread is there, but it's often crumbly and
uneven in quality, or soggy if made with rye flour.
The white bread, however, is out of this world.

What most Hungarians eat most of the time is
félbarna, which means half-brown, but is actually
white bread made with wheat flour. Other
popular white breads have maize or potato flour
mixed into them. Lots of rolls are eaten: a *zsemle*
is fairly soft and round with crumbly crust, while
a *kifli* is crescent-shaped and saltier.

Many people take the trouble to go to a traditional baker for their bread. American-style sliced bread is available in supermarkets, and even that seems to be a little better than the original.

Unlike most food in Hungary, much of the cheese is bland and uninteresting. Apparently, 60 percent of the cheese eaten is Trappist *(trappista)*, a dull, rubbery substance. However, deep-fried in a breadcrumb batter it turns magically into something delicious, served with tartar sauce.

Liptauer *(körözött)* is a spiced-up, homemade spread of curds made of ewe's milk, with paprika and chopped onion. Curds *(túró)* are the basis for many delightful Hungarian dishes, sweet and savory, including a little refrigerated chocolate bar called a *túró rudi*. Mr. Hershey, are you listening?

Smoked *karaván* cheese is pleasant, and so is the local Emmenthaler, known as *Pannónia*. Hungarian Cheddar, made in Pécs, is good only for cheeseburgers. *Parenyica*, however, is a pleasant, half-hard cheese, spun into a spiral and then slightly smoked. *Pálpusztai* has one of the most revolting smells of any cheese known to man—you have been warned!

Bacon is another field where Anglo-Saxon and Hungarian tastes differ. Hungarians think the fat is the important part of bacon, and often eat it raw, but heavily smoked, seeing the lean of the bacon as a necessary evil, liable to get stuck between your teeth. Take a short, sharp knife, a raw onion, a good piece of Hungarian fat bacon *(szalonna)*, a large wine and soda *(nagyfröccs)*, and if you're feeling extravagant, a big beef tomato. Nothing could be better for a summer evening meal—but don't tell your cardiologist.

Sour cream is a typical ingredient of many Hungarian dishes—it's used more often than fresh cream, in fact. The heavy, rich, brown bean and boiled-bacon soup known as *joka bableves* (a meal in itself) comes with a generous spoonful floating on top. Sour cream is also an ingredient of mushroom *paprikás*, a standby for vegetarians. But its enchantment is greatest in *tökfőzelék*. Made of shredded summer squash (vegetable marrow), this normally dull gourd is transformed into a delicacy by a thick, sour-cream sauce flavoured with spice paprika, onion, and chopped dill.

Sweetmeats

Hungarians are fond of crêpes *(palacsinta)*. The usual flavors are *túró*, cocoa, or jam. Restaurants like you to order a more elaborate concoction of walnut cream, raisins, rum, and chocolate sauce named after the early twentieth-century restaurateur Károly Gundel. At home, crêpes are often served in a pile, with everyone filling and rolling up their own.

Most hot, sweet dishes are treated as a main course in themselves. They may be quite simple: pasta with ground walnut or poppy seed, and icing sugar, for instance. *Fánk*, often served with apricot jam, are not dissimilar to doughnuts. *Vargabéles* is one of a number of substantial sweet dishes, in this case involving eggs, *túró*, a special pasta, sugar, and raisins. Strudel *(rétes)* may also be eaten as a main meal, the commonest fillings being sweetened cottage cheese, sour cherry, and apple. Pastries from a baker make excellent snacks with coffee.

The creations that have visitors' eyes popping out of their heads are the gâteaux and tortes. You won't find many in self-service grocery stores, however. Hungarians like the ones made by a qualified confectioner *(cukrász)* in a specialist shop, and seldom attempt to make them at home. There are countless outlets up and down the country, especially busy on weekend afternoons. At the pinnacle of the confectioner's profession, and of period interior design, are the *cafés-confiseries* of Budapest: the Gerbeaud, the Hauer, the New York, the Művész (handy for the

Opera), the Angelika, the Daubner, the Ruszwurm, and a recent recruit, the Gresham.

GOING TO RESTAURANTS

Although some suggestions have been made about where to go for a cake, it would be difficult to do the same for a meal. Restaurants come and go, and there's far too low a correlation between what you pay and the quality of the food or service. Even the few remaining Gypsy bands migrate from time to time, let alone the headwaiters and chefs on which everything depends. There are no reliable restaurant guides in print. Almost all the information in the publications purporting to be guides consists of advertisements, for which the restaurants pay.

Food and drink in Hungary, whether bought in a shop or consumed in a restaurant, with or without pretensions, will cost about half what it would from an equivalent outlet in Western Europe. But at the risk of sounding negative, here are some warnings. Avoid the Buda Castle District particularly and, to a lesser extent, downtown Pest. You'll find overpriced food, with overdramatic decor. (And the bread is likely to be stale.) Avoid that place with dim lighting that looks like a cross between a restaurant and a nightclub, particularly if there are single young ladies posing tastefully on some of the barstools. Don't go to hotel restaurants or others that obviously cater to tourists—they probably charge about 50 percent more than you would pay elsewhere. And don't bother with restaurants that purport to offer foreign cuisine. Very often they don't, or what they offer is an international hodgepodge, and there's a premium to pay. Even Indian restaurants are expensive. The only good value here is given by some of the Greek and Turkish kebab places.

Having said that, there are millions of good lunches waiting to be eaten—restaurant food in Hungary tends to be at its best around 1:00 p.m. After that, it's probably better to choose from the "freshly made" *(frissensültek)* section of the bill of fare rather than the "ready-made" *(készételek)*. Rice and pasta, for instance, will have lost much of their moisture content by mid-afternoon.

Consider having the set meal, confusingly known as the *menü*. This normally consists of soup, a smaller portion of a main course, and some kind of sweet dish, perhaps fruit or a slice of cake. This gets over one of the problems in Hungarian restaurants these days. There's tough competition for customers, and one competitive weapon that's used is outsized portions, so that many customers can't cope with more than the main course, whereas Hungarian food is meant to be enjoyed as a succession of dishes, not as one big plateful, like a dog's dinner.

Now, let's say you've been recommended a good restaurant. Hungarian etiquette dictates that the host should walk in first and attract the attention of the staff. Even in quite modest establishments, there'll be someone to show you to a table. By all means bargain over this and see if you can sit at the table that looks best. Two waiters will  come—one for the drinks and one for the food. Waiters' wine recommendations are usually serviceable and fair. Enjoy your meal, and don't be in any hurry. If it's dinner you're having, stay put all evening if you wish, ordering this and that from time to time.

Gypsy bands are out of fashion, but no visit to Hungary is really complete without one. They're fascinating to watch, especially the cimbalom—a vast concert dulcimer whose strings are struck with sticks like a xylophone. Any tune in the world can be converted into Hungarian Gypsy music at the drop of a hat. So as the night draws on, don't be shy about exhibiting your karaoke talents when the leader *(primás)* comes to your table and plays the number of your choice to your lady love.

A Winter's Day

A couple of days after Christmas we set out to see one of Hungary's buried treasures, and to find a good restaurant.

Once out of Budapest, we were almost on our own for a two-hour drive down a winding road, with the Balaton Uplands on our left. Then we reached the dusty, half-deserted little town of Sümeg. Our aim was to go into the parish church there, but it was locked. We wandered about, passing a dilapidated Baroque mansion and the local museum. An elderly lady asked us what we were looking for. We told her. "Oh, there he goes!" she cried, pointing to a tall young man carrying shopping bags—the sexton! Of course he would let us into the church and share with us his enthusiasm for the frescoes. There was just enough wintry light to see them.

The frescoes of Franz Anton Maulbertsch (1724–95) can't be transported to Paris or New York for exhibition. If they could, everyone would have heard of him. But perhaps it's better this way. His finest work is one of his earliest— Sümeg parish church (1757–9). Google "Maulbertsch Sumeg," and see for yourself.

We found half the town having a late lunch in a barn of a restaurant at the foot of Sümeg's medieval castle. We had an excellent meal.

IN YOUR CUPS

Elderly Australians who remember when the bars
in Victoria closed at six might enjoy visiting a
Hungarian *kocsma* (pub), *italbolt* (drink shop), or
borozó (wine bar), with its uniquely smoky, rancid
smell. They're not recommended to anyone else.
Beer, wine and the local spirit, *pálinka*, are drunk
by men at great speed, and that's that. No food.
Some villages have nothing else, mind you, so you
may need to go into one from time to time. Pay as
you drink. Most close about 9:00 p.m.

One step up the ladder is the *presszó*. This may
still have some pretensions as a place to have an
espresso coffee and eat a cake, but the main
business is drink. There is usually table service.
They come into their own in the summer, when
it's pleasant to sit outside. This is a broad category
and includes plenty of civilized places to drink or
meet your friends, unless the television's on too
loud. They stay open till 11:00 p.m. or later. Pay
the waitstaff when you leave, unless you're just
having a quickie at the counter.

A brasserie *(söröző)* sells beer and other drinks
and the kind of grilled food that's good after a
hard day's work. Cubicles in knotty pinewood
would be typical. One of these is probably the best
place to walk into with the family in a strange
town. Kitchens close about 9:00 p.m., but the
drinking goes on later.

TIPPING

The amount to tip is easy—10–15 percent of the bill, unless there's a (rare) service charge. More important is how to tip. Only one waiter can give bills—you'll notice the wallet in his trouser pocket—but you can ask any of the staff, "*Fizetni szeretnék*" ("I'd like to pay"). Unless you're out in the wilds, there will be some kind of printout to tell you the damage. Convincing and mechanized though this may look, it's worth checking a little more carefully than you might at home.

Having done so, add your percentage, round up the sum, and tell the waiter how much you're prepared to pay, including the tip. It's always better to pay in local currency than anything else. Most restaurants take Visa or MasterCard, but not all take American Express or Diners Club.

There's no need to tip other staff (there may be a small fixed charge to use the restroom). The exception is live music. The violinist who serenaded your loved one, or the pianist who obligingly played your favorite number, doesn't share the handout at the end of the day. About 1,000 forints is appropriate at present, inserted near the bridge of the violin or tucked behind the piano's open fallboard.

Drinking in Public

There is a law against drinking alcohol in the street and in various other public places in Hungary, enforced at the discretion of local authorities.

CAFÉ LIFE

Café life in the Austro-Hungarian sense has been undergoing a renaissance in Budapest and some other cities. The word to look for over the door is *kávé*, or *kávéhaz*. Expect large numbers of young people lingering over coffee and drinks and talking at the tops of their voices. Most cafés sell a limited range of food, competently cooked and served. Many stay open until the wee hours.

Of course, there are plenty of places that don't really fit into any of these categories. For a pleasant evening with friends, a modest restaurant is probably the most convenient and comfortable. Kitchens tend to close by 10:00 p.m., after which the waiters begin crumb-shaking rituals designed to speed the parting guests.

BOX OFFICE BARGAINS

Budapest is paradise for fans of opera, ballet, and classical music, the ticket prices are surprisingly low, and there are no extras apart from a tip of a couple of hundred forints at the cloakroom as you pick up your things when you leave.

Take the Opera (*Magyar Állami Operaház*)—one of the world's great late-nineteenth-century theater buildings, by the way. The original-language repertoire includes good doses of

Mozart, Verdi, Puccini, and Wagner, well sung by Hungarian and young foreign singers, sprinkled with lesser-known Hungarian greats (Erkel, Bartók, Ránki), well-chosen twentieth-century works (Janacek, Prokofiev, Shostakovich, Britten), and classical and modern ballets. Some productions are at the Erkel Theater, however, a monster of a place built in 1910–11.

The most expensive opera ticket is about 15,000 forints (U.S. $75) and the cheapest (certain seats for some matinees) 300 forints ($1.53). What Hungarians usually buy, though, are subscriptions for several performances, which offer price reductions and a chance to book the same seats year after year.

Visually, the best place in Budapest to listen to a symphony or choral music is the main hall of the Academy of Music (*Zeneakadémia*). The ambience, the gilt, the organ pipes, the proportions—all divine. The Vigadó, also late nineteenth century, was crudely restored in the 1970s and is far less exciting. The Budapest Convention Center (1980s) has dull acoustics. The brand-new National Concert Hall by the Danube has been well received.

The four main symphony orchestras in Budapest are the Hungarian Symphony (*Magyar Telekom Szimfonikus Zenekara*), the Hungarian Radio Symphony (*Magyar Rádió Szimfonikus Zenekara*), the Budapest Philharmonic (*Budapesti Filharmóniai Társaság Zenekara*), and the Budapest Festival Orchestra (*Budapesti Fesztiválzenekar*).There are other full-time orchestras in Debrecen, Győr, Miskolc, Pécs, Szeged, and Szombathely.

There are strong traditions of chamber music and chamber orchestral playing as well, so that hardly a night passes without a concert or a recital somewhere. Other good performances of interest to foreigners are given at the Operetta (operettas and musicals, but in Hungarian) and the Budai Vigadó (exuberant folk-dance shows).

GALLERIES AND MUSEUMS
There are three places in Budapest that art lovers mustn't miss. The first is the Museum of Fine Arts (*Szépművészeti Múzeum*), which has a fine

collection of European paintings. Three of the most famous exhibits are Raphael's *Esterházy Madonna*, Goya's *Girl Carrying Water*, and Delacroix's exquisite *Horse Frightened by Lightning*. Monet, Manet, Cézanne, Renoir, Gauguin, Chagall, Rembrandt, and many others are represented.

The second is the Hungarian National Gallery in Buda Castle, containing the works of Hungarian artists down the ages. Some of them are astonishingly good and are rarely exhibited outside the country. Of earlier masters, look especially for Miklós Barabás (1810–98), József Borsos (1821–83), Viktor Madarász (1830–1917), Mihály Munkácsy (1844–1900), and Tivadar Csontváry Kosztka (1853–1919), as well as avant-garde "activists" of the 1920s such as Béla Uitz (1887–1972) and Lajos Kassák (1887–1967).

The third place is the Opera building, completed in 1884. The frescoes that clothe most of the public areas are remarkable compositions by three masters of Hungarian historicism, Károly Lotz, Bertalan Székely, and Mór Than.

On the whole, museums and galleries in Hungary tend to be small and specialized. Collections of particular interest include the open-air sculpture park at Diósd, showing the Socialist Realist work of the Communist period, the Museum of Modern Art in Pécs, the Museum of Naive Artists in Kecskemét, the Victor Vasarely

Collection in Óbuda, the Catholic collections in Esztergom, and the Serbian one in Szentendre.

TIME FOR A SWIM

There are lots of wonderful places to bathe in Hungary. Three of the best are a bathing and swimming complex, a natural thermal lake, and a beach beneath an extinct volcano.

Budapest's Császár-Komjádi complex (II. Árpád fejedelem útja 8., known locally as the *Csaszi*) dates from Turkish times. It contains the best pools for serious swimmers. There are five pools, three in the open air. The Császár has the Turkish baths, while the Lukács is a delightful nineteenth-century establishment.

The Healing Lake (*Gyógy-tó*) at Hévíz, near Lake Balaton, is 130 feet (39.5 m) deep and the second-largest thermal lake in the world. The slightly radioactive water changes every two days, but remains at least 80°F (27°C) at the surface. This is a chance to swim among red tropical water lilies below Victorian bathhouses.

The third tip is to relax in the silky water of Balaton off the beach at Szigliget and gaze up at the extinct volcano of Badacsony, where the best wines of the region grow. Then you can sample the wines and fried Balaton fish—try the *fogas* (pike-perch)— at any of a dozen restaurants.

chapter **seven**

TRAVELING

PUBLIC TRANSPORTATION

Hungary has a dense system of public transportation, of not a very high standard. The buses go too fast for comfort and the trains are too slow. It's common for buses, streetcars, and trains to be late, dirty, crowded, or cancelled—but the fares are low.

Hungarian State Railways (MÁV), the monopoly train company, has a mainly radial network of just below 5,000 miles (8,000 km), centered on Budapest. The Intercity services to eight major cities are cleaner, faster, and more reliable (and more expensive) than others. Long-distance bus services run by the Volán group of companies, each a monopoly in its own area, augment the train services but cost 40–50 percent more.

Train or bus tickets must be bought before boarding, from a ticket office open, by phone, or on the Internet (http://elvira.hu).

Budapest's Western *(Nyugati)* and Eastern *(Keleti)* railway termini are remarkable pieces of nineteenth-century architecture. The former was designed by the Eiffel company and completed in 1877. The old station restaurant with its ornate cast ironwork is probably the most elegant branch of McDonald's in Europe.

Water transportation is more limited. There are passenger services upstream from Budapest on the Danube and on Lake Balaton between spring and autumn. The hydrofoil up the Danube to Vienna is also popular.

Nearly all commercial flights land or take off from one of the three terminals of Budapest Ferihegy Airport. There are no scheduled internal passenger flights in Hungary.

Punch and Ride

Budapest's public transportation system is as eclectic as the city's architecture: buses, streetcars, trolleybuses, suburban trains, underground railways (three lines radiating from downtown Deák tér), a funicular, a rack railway, a chairlift (up the Buda Hills), and a narrow-gauge children's railway.

For local public transportation, passengers need to buy individual tickets, a book of tickets, or a pass before boarding. Tickets must be validated on boarding the vehicle. In Budapest, this means pushing the ticket—with its grid of numbers in front and facing up—into a slot for punching or canceling. This has to be done at the station barrier on the Budapest Metro. Gruff inspectors levy spot fines on those they catch without a valid ticket.

The funicular runs from Clark Ádám tér at the Buda end of the Chain Bridge up to the Royal Palace of Buda. It's expensive, but the view's good.

The underground railway line M1 was the first on continental Europe when it opened on May 2, 1896, and Emperor-King Francis Joseph himself had a ride six days later.

An interesting trip for transportation enthusiasts is to take the rack railway *(fogaskerekű)* from Városmajor, two tram stops from Moszkva

tér, up Sváb-hegy. This opened in 1874. It proceeds rather slowly and noisily up 4,082 yards (3,733 m) of steep gradient in about fifteen minutes. It's then a short walk to the terminus of the Children's Railway *(gyermekvasút)*, for a brief ride through the woods to Hűvösvölgy: trains depart at least every hour in the summer and occasionally in winter. Built in 1948, the railway is run by child volunteers in immaculate railway uniforms. Budapest's most scenic tram route, the

56, will take you back from Hűvösvölgy to
Moszkva tér in about twenty minutes.

TAXIS

If you want to take a taxi, most people agree that
branded taxis (Főtaxi, phone 222 2222, City Taxi,
211 1111, etc.) are more reasonable, reliable, and
honest than lone wolves. The complicated tariffs
work out at about 350–500 forints per km
($1.70–2.40), depending on distance and brand of
taxi. Add a small roundup tip of up to 10 percent.
Good deals can be struck for half-day or day trips.

DRIVING

The main highways in Hungary are maintained
by the state, including the 391 miles (630 km)
of expressway. If all goes well, there will be 597
miles (960 km) of them by the end of 2006.
The rest of the 19,000 miles (30,000 km) of
roads belong to local or regional government
authorities. You have to pay to use almost all
expressways, except the M0 bypassing
Budapest, through a system of tickets valid for
the network.

The minimum age for a driver's license is
seventeen, but most car rental companies insist
on twenty-one and a license held for more than

a year. European licenses are valid in Hungary, but visitors from most non-European countries, including the U.S.A., Canada, and Australia, must have an International Driver's Permit.

Hungary uses the international system of road signs and markings common throughout Europe, although these may be poorly maintained. The same applies to the road surface, especially in cities. One important rule that may be unfamiliar calls on drivers to give way to the right at unmarked junctions (the so-called "right-hand rule"). Trams have priority at all times.

Low-beam headlights are compulsory even in the daytime outside built-up areas. Full headlights are prohibited in built-up areas at night. A first-aid kit and a warning triangle must be carried in the car. The main speed limits are 31 mph (50 kmph) in built-up areas (within the black-on-white city-limit signs), 56 mph (90 kmph) outside built-up areas, 68 mph (110 kmph) on limited-access trunk roads, and 80 mph (130 kmph) on freeways. There are pay-and-display parking systems in Budapest and many other towns.

Police may stop a car for no apparent reason, and find ingenious reasons to levy fines. They do so by giving the driver a yellow ticket for a sum to be paid at a post office. There is a system of black marks, so that successive offenses, even minor ones, may lead to confiscation of the driver's license. The blood alcohol limit is zero.

When an accident occurs, the police must be called if there is personal injury, or if the drivers involved can't agree on who is to blame. Otherwise the drivers simply exchange insurance documents or reach a private agreement.

EMERGENCY NUMBERS

Fire/police/ambulance 112

The Automobile Club 188

OUT FOR THE DAY

It is worth mentioning a few excursion destinations out of Budapest. Wherever you go, take time to sit and eat in a local restaurant—they're usually remarkably cheap, even compared with Budapest. The same applies to private accommodation, which is plentiful.

By public transportation, you can visit **Szentendre** (quaint streets, Serbian churches, Serbian museum, art); **Esztergom** (basilica, churches, Christian museum, castle ruins, and eighteenth-century town); **Vácrátót** (vast, unkempt botanical gardens); **Gödöllő** (royal summer house); **Kecskemét** (Art Nouveau architecture, toy museum, and naive art); and **Herend** (porcelain factory and museum).

If you have a car, try **Hollókő** (traditional village, folk costume) and **Szécsény** (a leaning church tower, mansion with a hunting museum, and the quintessential country town); **Eger** (Hungary's best Baroque town, Lyceum, basilica, castle, and churches); **Pécs** (art galleries, Baroque buildings, and Turkish remains); **Keszthely** (Balaton resort, Georgikon, palace) and **Sümeg** (church frescoes, castle); **Majk** (eighteenth-century hermitage) and **Várgesztes** (castle); and **Sopron** (medieval town, museums, forests).

The young will enjoy **Szentendre** outskirts (open-air museum); **Visegrád** (ruined palaces and castles, Danube views, summer bob—bobsleighs with wheels); **Ipolytarnóc** (23,000,000-year-old fossils and footprints in the back of beyond); **Szilvásvárad** (Lipizzaner stud farm, carriage museum, waterfalls, and hikes); **Aggtelek** (a vast cave system that extends into Slovakia), **Hortobágy** (horsemanship and

wide open spaces); **Balatonfüred** (bathing, boating, and Balaton shipping); and **Tihany** (views, cottages, and an abbey).

HEALTH AND SECURITY

Crime against the person is low in Hungary, even by European standards. The commonest problems for visitors are pickpockets and thefts from vehicles. Police are normally helpful to tourists, but knowledge of English is not found in every police station, and you may have to take a Hungarian-speaker with you to report a crime. ID (a passport or driver's license with a photograph) should be carried at all times. Among the offenses most commonly committed by foreigners in Hungary are driving under the influence of alcohol (as we have seen, the permitted blood alcohol limit is zero) and other traffic offenses. Seek legal advice immediately if more than a small fine is at stake.

The health service suffers from uneven standards of provision and the morale of health staff is poor, yet private medical insurance or services have scarcely made any inroads. E.U. citizens are entitled to free medical care, and other foreigners to emergency care. The gratuities that Hungarians routinely slip to doctors are not expected from foreign patients.

chapter eight

BUSINESS BRIEFING

Before considering the kind of place Hungary is for business today, let's begin with some hard facts. They are hard for Hungary and they are hard for people doing business here—but they're not as hard as they were.

THE ECONOMY

Look at it this way. Hungary ranks 109th among the countries of the world in territory, 80th in population, and 62nd in GDP, the commonest measure of the size of an economy. So in world terms, it's developed, but in European terms, it's not. Between 1990 and about 1995, Hungary made the painful transition from a centrally planned Communist economy to a capitalist market one. It involved wholesale privatization, mass redundancies, deep recession, and bitter controversy, but it seems to have been worth it.

Hungary went on to hit some remarkable annual rates of economic growth. (They can best be expressed in GDP per head at purchasing-power parity—PPP—which cuts out the idiosyncrasies of currency exchange rates.) Growth averaged 3.71 percent over the 1995–2004 period, while the then fifteen members of the E.U. were averaging only 1.58 percent.

But there's still plenty of catching up to do. Hungary's GDP per head in 2004 was only U.S. $14,900 (at PPP, remember—about half that in nominal terms), as opposed to the U.K. $29,600 and the U.S. $40,100, and an average of $26,900 in the 25 current E.U. members.

One factor behind Hungary's success was an early lead over the other post-Communist countries in attracting foreign investment. It built up a stock of foreign direct investment (FDI) of $1,818 per head between 1990 and 1999, as opposed to $1,406 for the Czech Republic and $776 for Poland. This flow of inward investment leveled off between 2000 and 2003 (an FDI per head increment of $901, as opposed to $2,060 for the Czech Republic and $590 for Poland).

One reason why investors smiled on Hungary in the 1990s was that it was relatively quick to install legislation and institutions to safeguard their interests. It also had a feisty little private sector, although how much help that was is debated. And foreigners seemed to prefer the Hungarian privatization approach: *selling off* state assets, rather than making periodic handouts to citizens, as many post-Communist countries did.

The result is an economy with a big private sector (generating 70.9 percent of GDP in 2002) and a high proportion of foreign ownership. According to recent figures, more than 43 percent of Hungary's commercial earnings (gross value added) come from firms in full or part-foreign ownership. That share is 66 percent in manufacturing industry and 87 percent in vehicle and component manufacturing.

SOCIAL OR UNSOCIAL

"I look upon that man, be him what he will, that endeavours to evade the payment of his just share of taxes, to be a robbing of every other member of the community that contributes his quota." Those words were written in 1763 by Thomas Turner, a shopkeeper of East Hoathly, in the English county of Sussex. Most Britons and North Americans, and almost all Scandinavians, would agree. Most Hungarians wouldn't.

The story of financial policy in the last fifteen years has been one of trying to balance the government books and of trying to make the tax system conform to the requirements of the E.U., which Hungary eventually joined in May 2004. But the real struggle has been against social flair and ingenuity.

For example, there has been a long battle to ensure that waiters, hairdressers, and others such as the medical profession (yes, really) pay at least some tax on the tips they receive. Then there are the many self-employed Hungarians—though employed in an economic sense, working for one "customer" on a regular basis—who have started a small company with their spouse and pay themselves a minimum wage.

Such things gather a momentum and logic of their own, but there is some economic sense behind the urge to add a firm as an extra member of so many Hungarian families. Currently, the top income tax rate is 38 percent, while the top rate of corporate income tax is 16. Ostensibly, this can save both sides a lot in welfare contributions and other payroll and income taxes; but in fact the tax savings for the members of these "deposit partnerships" *(Bt.)* may be hardly enough to pay the accountant.

The Hungarians are gradually being coaxed into the tax system. Among recent recruits have been peasant farmers (no E.U. subsidies unless you register for tax, my man) and small firms who go for a flat-rate turnover tax called EVA in return for exemption from VAT.

GOVERNMENT BY SURPRISE

This is not to say that government behavior has always been rational or honest. Perhaps we don't want to go too deeply into the question of corruption here. Accusations are easily made and difficult to prove. Let's just say that Hungary scored 4.8 out of 10 in one recent "world corruption index"—equal with Italy, cleaner than South Africa and South Korea, but beaten by Costa Rica and a host of Arab countries, and way behind the United States (7.5) and the U.K. (8.6).

Some Hungarian officials may not be shy about lining their pockets, conforming to Communist tradition. But, equally, some eminent international firms have tarnished their reputations and had initially successful tender applications overturned by the courts recently because their dealings were not aboveboard.

Perhaps more important to the business climate is the package of surprises that comes into force on January 1 each year: the state budget. Stability in the tax and accounting system seems as elusive as ever.

Hungary has come through an orgy of conforming to E.U. rules, but the talk on both sides of Parliament is still of "budget reform." The present government has been implementing a program of a hundred little steps leading up to the general elections in 2006. Nothing to write home about individually, but most call for a business response of some kind, and presumably many will turn out to be too costly once the elections are out of the way and will be reversed or altered again.

More surprises: every general election since 1990 has produced a coalition of a different political complexion from the last, and of course, from the image its members presented of themselves beforehand. There's been a series of four-yearly "changes of system," when ministry officials you may have grown used to have lost their jobs, and bringing a host of bright new fiscal and regulatory schemes to adapt to. So keep your commercial seat belts on for the time being.

BUSINESS RELATIONSHIPS

Hungarians doing business think in terms of relationships—with their colleagues, their superiors, and their customers and suppliers, as individuals. Historically, this has a lot to do with the Communist system and its aftermath, which left only personal relationships intact. For you, the foreign businessperson, it brings a need to identify a single person in a partner firm, to whom you relate and with whom you do business. He or she will deal with the rest, where possible. If your link isn't there, don't expect anyone to stand in. Your file will patiently await his or her return, which will be annoying if you're in a hurry.

Hierarchy
The structure of a firm in Hungary is hierarchical. This means decision making takes time. You may have agreed to something with your partner, only to find the decision unexpectedly overruled higher up.

Where talks are being conducted with a team of Hungarian negotiators, the ones who do the talking may be the ones who speak the best English, rather than the most senior. Your eye contact will tend to be with the leader of the group. Where it's uncertain who is the leader, it will have to be divided fairly equally, at least until it emerges who's doing the talking.

It's often the case that you discuss everything and seem to be reaching agreement, but no one in the room is qualified to clinch the deal. So it's extremely valuable to know something about the team beforehand. Job descriptions on visiting cards are a start, of course, but inquiries can be made of earlier contacts in the firm or secretarial staff while you're waiting. This is not classified information.

Good Manners

Many Anglo-Saxon business customs are a puzzle or an irritant to Hungarians, though less to the young business-school graduate than to their parents, but it's worth minimizing such behavior. Personal lateness or last-minute changes to schedules put them out.

When you visit someone's office, shake hands all around, introduce yourself, and sit down only when invited. Be restrained in your body language: don't stretch, or spread your limbs over the furniture, don't fidget or do finger-clicking exercises, and don't pace up and down, explaining vehemently, with your hands in your pockets. Take any opportunity to compliment your hosts on their premises, their furniture, the town, the district, the view. If you are offered some refreshment, accept it. This is the time to relax a little and build up the personal relations that mean so much to Hungarians. Don't show impatience if the meeting is interrupted. Hungarian executives must keep several balls in the air at once.

A visiting businesswomen will find a scarcity of women in positions of authority in Hungary. She may consider the courtesies of her Hungarian hosts to be old-fashioned, but they should be accepted with politeness and respect.

Hungarians may confuse Anglo-Saxon informality with insolence. Hierarchy again: if

you are insufficiently polite, it may appear to the
Hungarian that you're underestimating his or her
status. If you should receive someone in your own
office, stand up, apologize if you're on the
telephone, offer a comfortable seat, and sit down
with your guest away from the desk. Offer some
token hospitality—coffee, say, or mineral water.

It's always worth remembering how reluctant
Hungarians are to do business with someone
they don't like. A pleasant, sympathetic
approach is extremely valuable, because it
breeds confidence in your potential partners.
Condescension, on the other hand, doesn't work
well at all, as many Western business advisers
found when they were flown in after the
collapse of Communism. Be charming and
attentive, and avoid shows of irritation—if you
want to do a deal, that is.

SERVICE WITH A SNORT

Having painted a picture of old-world courtesy in
business offices, it has to be said that at a lower
commercial level, for example in shops, many
Hungarians are abrupt with their customers. Not
so long ago this was a shortage economy, where
shop staff had the power to provide or withhold.
But sloppy service also reflects low levels of staff

training, pay, and status, and preconceived, simplistic ideas of how a deal should go: here it is, let the customers take it or leave it.

It's not just the service. Many suppliers keep no stocks worth mentioning. You can order a computer system, say, at quite a good price, and the supplier can order it from the wholesaler. But you're likely to be buying a pig in a poke. There's no chance to look at it before you buy, let alone try it out. Often dealers themselves are poorly informed. It's up to the customers to interpret the technical details and see if they fit their needs. They are the ones who need the expertise in the world of Hungarian purchasing.

One key commercial concept lacking in many small and even medium-sized Hungarian firms is the repeat order. Where will the firm be by the time you need your next car, or insurance policy, or lakeside apartment let? The company is undercapitalized, and needs your money now. Buy, or stop wasting its time.

So what happens if you buy something that's faulty? Oddly enough, there aren't many problems if you have proof of purchase. Troubleshooting is something that many Hungarians seem to enjoy. The real trouble arrives when undercapitalized firms start giving ten-year maintenance guarantees—on a new apartment, for example.

CONTRACTS AND FULFILLMENT

Sellers, contractors, and providers in Hungary pay little attention to deadlines. Penalty clauses may be included in the contract, but they're often treated as if they themselves were up for repeated renegotiation. Let's forget the penalty clause for another couple of weeks and we'll have the work done by then, they suggest, hoping you don't have the energy to dismiss them and find someone else.

The heart of the matter lies in contractual relations. First, the spoken word doesn't constitute an undertaking of any kind in Hungarian business. At best, it means "I like the idea and I'll see how it goes." A contract in Hungary is not a contract until it's been negotiated, drawn up in due form, and signed and stamped before witnesses, best of all before a notary. Even then, if it turns out to be detrimental or inconvenient to one party, that party could ignore it.

Doing business successfully, after all, rests on considerations that go beyond a specific contract—honesty, trust, reputation, and the prospect of future business relations. Hungarian business is all too often thwarted by short-termism: cynical reliance on the fact that pursuing small claims through the courts is expensive and time-consuming—there's no equivalent of the U.K. simplified small-claims proceedings here.

Lost Opportunities

When Suzuki, GM, Ford, and later Volkswagen-Audi decided to bring chunks of their manufacturing to Hungary in the 1990s, they were full of assurances about local content. They looked forward to working not only with Hungarian labor, but also with Hungarian suppliers and subcontractors. But, because some suppliers proved unreliable—in many cases due to undercapitalization— and there were fewer applicants than they expected, that didn't happen.

Hungarians had wondered at the time whether these promises weren't a bit too good to be true. Yet it's hard to impugn the motives of these car companies, because what they actually did involved them in great management effort—greater than they had envisaged. To meet their local-content obligations, they had to persuade their existing, foreign suppliers to follow them into Hungary and supply them reliably from here.

Today, 87 percent of the gross value added by the vehicle manufacturing sector is made by firms with a foreign stake in them. The contribution of Hungarian small or medium-sized subcontractors is minute.

CRONIES AND CREATIVITY

Faced with the remaining inherited shortcomings of the business environment, Hungarians have two lines of defense. One is cronyism. Whatever cronyism may be in other parts of the world, it's plain business sense here. Although foreigners in Hungary are short of relatives and old classmates, who make the best cronies of all, they too can start picking up friends and involving them in their business.

The other line of defense Hungarians use is good news indeed: they prefer to deal with foreign firms. And that means you. Your reputation for reliability and honesty has preceded you, giving you an important competitive advantage. Provided you don't chew gum in the managing director's office, of course.

Finally, a further piece of good news: Hungarians have some valuable business virtues.

- They are born interdisciplinarians, seldom taking a narrow "engineer's" view.
- They are intrigued by new technologies and methods.
- They are excellent at solving a problem or coping in a crisis. This ability to make things work against all the odds kept Hungary ahead of the other Central and East European countries in the Communist and the post-Communist transition periods.
- They are often prepared to go far beyond the call of duty once their imagination has been fired.

These virtues may be some of the reasons why young Hungarian executives have been notably successful with the international corporations that dominate the Hungarian manufacturing, commercial, and banking and financial-service sectors these days.

It's a bit like Hungarian soccer players, really. Free them from the shackles of Hungarian management and they'll score goals for you every time.

chapter **nine**

COMMUNICATING

THE HUNGARIAN LANGUAGE

The Hungarian language belongs to the Finno-Ugric language family. These languages are found in the Carpathian Basin, in Eastern Scandinavia, and in pockets across Eastern Europe and Siberia. They are the native languages of about 25 million people. Only Hungarian (*Magyar*), Finnish, and Estonian are official languages of states. Sami (Lappish) languages have local official status in Norway, Sweden, and Finland, as do some other Finno-Ugric languages in the Russian Federation.

Hungarian is spoken as a native language by 14.5 million people, of which ten million live in Hungary. It is an isolated language, insofar as the main languages in all neighboring countries belong to other language families—Slavic (Slovak, Ukrainian, Serbian, Croatian, and Slovenian), Germanic (German), and Romance (Romanian)—so there is little structural similarity, even if some vocabulary is shared.

Hungarian vocabulary comes from several sources. Although Hungarian contains only about 700 Finno-Ugric root elements, 60 percent of its vocabulary and an average of about 80 percent of any literary text are of Finno-Ugric origin. So Hungarian is Finno-Ugric to a much greater extent than English is Germanic—only about 25 percent of words in modern English derive from Old English or Old Norse.

In prehistoric times, there were strong Turkic and Iranic influences on Hungarian. Since the Hungarians settled in the Carpathian Basin at the end of the ninth century, many words and expressions have entered the language from Latin, Ottoman Turkish, German, Greek, and Slav languages, and more recently, French and English.

Some English loan words in Hungarian have acquired different meanings. *Szmoking* means a tuxedo and *winchester* a computer hard drive, for instance. Among the commonest words of Hungarian origin in English are biro (ballpoint pen, from *Bíró*, the name of its Hungarian-born inventor), and coach (from Kocs, a Hungarian cart-making village). Goulash, the typical souplike stew of Hungary, gets its name from *gulyás*, a cowherd. Then there's hussar (*huszár*, itself of Slav origin), itsy-bitsy *(ici-pici)*, and paprika (the Hungarian word for capsicum).

PRONUNCIATION

Achieving an understandable pronunciation of
Hungarian is no problem for most English
speakers. There are three general points.

English tends to blur the distinction between
the *length* of a syllable and its *stress* or lack of it.
These are quite distinct in Hungarian. The main
stress always goes on the first syllable of a word.

Short vowels *(a, e, i, o, u)* are distinct from long
(á, é, í, ó, ú). There are also modified vowels, *ö, ő,
ü,* and *ű,* pronounced as in *Löwe* in German and
tu in French, short and long.

Long and short consonants are also clearly
distinguished: *tt* is pronounced as in *set tea,* not as
in *pretty, nn* as in *ten nuts,* not as in *penny.*

Hungarians think their language is written
phonetically, and this is an assumption that
foreigners struggling with Hungarian names and
expressions can live with. Here's a table of
troublesome letters and letter combinations. The
others are pronounced in a similar way to English.

Hungarian	Near English equivalent	
a	o	as in pot*
á	a	as in father
c	ts	as in pots
cs	ch	as in chop
dzs	j	as in jet

Hungarian	Near English equivalent	
e	e	as in pet
é	ai	as in paid**
g	g	as in got
gy	d	as in during
i	i	as in pit
í	ee	as in meet
j	y	as in yet
ly	y	as in yet
ny	n	as in new*
o	o	(with a round mouth)
ó	aw, oo	as in paw,* too
ö	a	as in about
ő	u	as in purple*
r	r	(trilled)
s	sh	as in shot
sz	s	as in spot
ty	t	as in tune*
u	u	as in put
ú	oo	as in boot
ü	ü	(as German, short)
ű	ü	(as German, long)
zs	s	as in pleasure

* = British pronunciation is nearer
** = American pronunciation is nearer

GESTURES

Although Hungarians' body language is similar to that of other Central and Northern Europeans, there are some differences in the gestures they use. Here are some of the more usual ones:

- *Counting*—starts with the thumb.
- *Pointing*—to something is done with the forefinger, but pointing the way is done with the flat of the hand.
- *Beckoning*—with all the fingers of the hand.
- *Approval*—a circle of forefinger and thumb.
- *Doubt*—the back of the hand, all fingers extended, is rocked from side to side.
- *I don't know*—shrug the shoulders with palms up. This is not dismissive as such, as it might seem in Britain or the U.S.A.

THE MEDIA

Newspaper readership in Hungary is high. There are four quality national dailies *(Népszabadság, Magyar Nemzet, Népszava,* and *Magyar Hírlap),* three national tabloids (one of them free) and four specialist dailies (business, sports). But people outside Budapest are more likely to read one of the twenty-four county dailies. There

are two weekly papers in English and one in German, all published in Budapest.

Almost all dailies and most periodicals are foreign-owned, but editorial interference from abroad is unusual.

Of the five national television channels, three are publicly owned and two foreign-owned. The three main national public radio stations are complemented by countless private local stations. There are no foreign-language stations at present, but broadcasts from neighboring countries can be picked up easily in some parts of Hungary. Cable TV is widely available, often with alternative packages that include English, French, Spanish, and German stations. The biggest of around 500 cable TV providers are UPC Magyarország (30 percent) and T-Kábel (10 percent).

MAIL SERVICES
Hungarian post offices (marked *Posta* in a green and red livery) usually open at 8:00 or 9:00 a.m. But the hours of operation vary. Some of them may close for lunch at some time between 12:00 noon and 2:00 p.m. They may close as early as 4:00 p.m. or as late as 7:00 p.m. Nearly all are closed on weekends. You can also buy stamps or postcards at a tobacconist or news vendor.

There are mailboxes in front of post offices and elsewhere in streets. Hungarians distrust these, and prefer to hand their mail over the counter. You need to do this anyway if you want a registered or priority service.

The post office has a monopoly of letter and newspaper deliveries. The newspaper usually arrives, but the ostensibly daily deliveries of letters are erratic. However, the delivery person also brings sums of money in cash, such as pensions and benefits. Post-office banking is efficient, but the range of services is limited.

Package and courier services are available, but these are no longer a post-office monopoly.

Postcodes
Every address in Hungary has a four-figure postcode, the digit denoting one of nine main areas. Budapest addresses begin with 1, for instance. Some other countries have four-figure postal codes, and for Hungary the prefix H– (e.g., H–1028) can be used to avoid confusion.

TELEPHONE AND INTERNET
The largely German-owned Magyar Telekom is the dominant telephone provider in Hungary, providing near-monopoly landline services in most areas of the country. Alternative call providers have

made little progress. The country's largest Internet and cell phone providers are part of the Magyar Telekom group. However, there is effective competition in the market for those two services. Competition for cable television comes only from airborne or direct satellite services.

The three nationwide cell phone providers use 1800 Hz GSM, so U.S. GSM users will need a dual-band phone for roaming. Hungarians are keen users of the SMS text messaging facility that GSM includes. All three companies put out a bewildering variety of opaque charging schemes.

However, prices of telecom and Internet services have followed world trends downward, after a time lag. DSL broadband in Hungary is normally asymmetric, that is, with faster downloads than uploads. Customer service in these areas has been improving and is normally available in English as well as Hungarian.

Cell phone services (approaching one cell phone per person over the age of six) are reaching the saturation point, but there has been media anxiety about the Internet spreading more slowly than in other European countries. However, numbers are approaching a million, with over half of the connections broadband, and a year-on growth rate of almost 20 percent in 2005, when there were eighty-seven different providers.

CONCLUSION

Why do so many foreign visitors fall in love with Hungary? Well, the first reason must be the Hungarians themselves, who are vivacious, amusing, inventive, and well-disposed toward foreigners. Those qualities make integration, even for a few days, a very pleasant and easy process for people of all ages. Hungarians have a sense of loyalty to their country and its assets that soon inspires newcomers too. It's also something worth cultivating. Hungarian books are worth reading, paintings worth viewing, and music worth hearing.

The climate is agreeable for nine months of the year, and there are ample opportunities for cultural, sporting, and outdoor activities. Some of the finest things in life—wining and dining—are good bargains. The pitfalls—shortcomings in infrastructure and service, visible social deprivation, slow bureaucracy—may be irritating, but they aren't usually dangerous.

The key to a rewarding stay in Hungary is to make friends, for friendship is the stuff of Hungarian society. This book will give you an added boost to making them—not that it's difficult, for an encounter with Hungary and its people is something that the visitor will never forget, and never regret.

Further Reading

Barber, Annabel. *Visible Cities. Budapest.* London/Budapest: Somerset Books, 2003.

Braham, Randolph. *The Politics of Genocide. The Holocaust in Hungary.* Detroit, MI: Wayne State UP, 2000.

Gorman, Gerard. *The Birds of Hungary.* London: Christopher Helm, 1996.

Kertész, Imre. *Fatelessness.* New York/London: Vintage, 2004. Nobel Prize novel.

Litván, György, ed. *The Hungarian Revolution of 1956. Reform, Revolt and Revolution 1953–1963.* New York /London: Longman, 1996.

Longley, Norm. *The Rough Guide to Hungary.* London: Rough Guides, 2005.

Molnár, Miklós. *A Concise History of Hungary.* Cambridge: CUP, 2001.

Shea, Christina. *Frommer's Budapest and the Best of Hungary.* Hoboken, NJ: Wiley, 2004.

Statistical Yearbook of Hungary 2004. Budapest: HCSO, 2005.

In-Flight Hungarian. New York: Living Language, 2001.

Further Browsing

http://dict.sztaki.hu/index.jhtml. Hungarian–English, English–Hungarian dictionaries.

http://www.hungarotips.com/hungarian/. Language lessons.

http://www.budapestinfo.hu/en/. Arts events, what's on calendar.

http://www.filolog.com/crossculture.html. Culture, manners, business, daily life.

http://www.libsci.sc.edu/bob/class/clis748/Studentwebguides/fall02/Hungary.htm. Broad business information, not all free.

http://www.magyarorszag.hu/angol. Good general information.

http://www.rev.hu/index_en.html. 1956 Revolution and history since the Second World War.

culture smart! hungary

Index

Acknowledgments

The author is most grateful to Áron Szőcs and Aliz McLean for their
research assistance, and to Zsófia Lászlo for reading the manuscript and
suggesting many valuable improvements. He also thanks Éva Ehrlich,
Győző and Miklós Ferencz, Klára Fóti, Anna Hernádi, Anikó Mágori,
Orsolya Mészáros, John and Éva Penney, Attila Szakolczai, and Elizabeth
Szász for their invaluable help, advice, and information.